Gods of Corruption

Attention Authors

'We Convert Fighters into Writers'. That's the motto of Manas Publications for more than four decades. Our message to the world is that India can win the battle not only by the bullet but also by the pen. There is no dearth of intellectuals in our country, but their knowledge is confined to them only. No sincere effort has been made by any other publisher to channelise their knowledge in national interest. That is why the talent of a large number of intellectuals remains latent. An author transforms his knowledge into a manuscript, and it is our job to spread his/her knowledge by converting it into a beautiful book. For over four decades, Manas has been motivating the intellectuals by publishing their manuscripts and would like to publish your manuscript too. If you or your colleagues have any manuscript ready for publication or are working on it, kindly contact us with detailed synopsis and list of contents. We will transform your work into a valuable publication. If you wish, we can also suggest you the suitable subjects for writing the books related to your area of expertise. Manas is known for its publishing quality and commitments. We take utmost care in production and give wide publicity to the book as well as its author through our national and international distribution network.

Gods of Corruption

Promilla Shankar
IAS (Retd)

Manas Publications
(We Convert Fighters into Writers)
New Delhi-110002 (INDIA)

MANAS PUBLICATIONS

(Publishers for IAS, IPS, IFS, IRS, Defence, Press, Judges etc.)
(Publishers, Distributors, Importers & Exporters)

4402/5-A, Ansari Road (Opp. HDFC Bank)
Darya Ganj, New Delhi-110 002 (India)
Off. 23260783, 23265523, Res. 23842660
Fax: 011-23272766
E-mail: manaspublications@gmail.com
manaspublications@yahoo.com

Website: www.manaspublications.in

ISBN 978-81-7049-507-9

₹ 595/-

Designed at
Manas Publications

Printed in India at
R.K. Print Service, Delhi and published by
Mrs Suman Lata for
Manas Publications, 4402/5-A, Ansari Road,
(Opp. HDFC Bank),
Darya Ganj, New Delhi-110 002 (INDIA)

For

My Grandsons

KARTHIKEYAN

&

AGASTYA

Preface

I JOINED the Indian Administrative Service (IAS) in 1976. There were not very many job options available to our generation. You either became an engineer, a teacher, a doctor or joined the Civil Services. Today the world is open for youngsters. They can go into any field, be it music, sport, designing, script writing or anything else. This was not the case in our time. Driven by idealism to serve the public, I joined the Civil Services and was allotted to the Uttar Pradesh cadre.

This book has been written with the express purpose of informing the public in general and young aspirants to the Civil Services in particular, as to the hard reality of the Civil Service. I was recently inducted as an advisor on the interview board for recruiting these youngsters. I was surprised by the number of youngsters who appear before the interview boards and say that they want to work for the downtrodden and help make a difference in the country. These were the same ideas with which, I too, entered the service in 1976 but having now retired after a tenure spanning 36 years, I will say that in UP, I could not make much of a difference. Whenever I tried to make a difference I was shunted out unceremoniously and even if I did manage to bring about some changes, they were soon reversed after my shift from that department.

The lesson I learnt from my years in the Civil Service was that in the Civil Service, as I presume in other professions too, to be successful you must be a cog in the wheel. If you want to do something new and think out of the box you will very likely upset the apple cart, which is not appreciated and consequently you will face the wrath of your masters. You must at all times ensure that the status-quo is not disturbed. You must not create work or challenges for anyone. You have to reaffirm the misplaced sense of the people in control that everything is under control. You must never be seen to have an independent mind.

You must be a sycophant. What work you do is not of as much importance as you hovering around your boss and saying yes to everything he or she says. I realized that IAS officers themselves do not want an upright and strong IAS officer to work with them. They prefer someone who is from the Provincial Civil Service whom they feel are more mature which in effect, means that they are more malleable. You must be ready to compromise and find via medias to circumvent rules and to find loopholes.

It is also surprising how soon young idealistic candidates, who join the service learn the ropes of getting along in their careers and change so much. It seems that the ideals stated in the interview are merely for sounding right with the Interview

Board. Civil servants have lost the nerve to disagree and put forward their own point of view. When they see the boss holding a certain point of view they clam shut. In fact they try and anticipate what the boss would like them to do. It is these tendencies that have brought the nation to this deplorable state.

Most of the problems that the officers face are from fellow officers and politicians. Everybody's thinking and views are different. They come with their own baggage and have all sorts of expectations from their subordinates. The most important thing one has to learn is to handle the boss as a professional environment is sorely lacking.

I have recorded some episodes from my career in this book. I would say that my 'shortcomings' were firstly that I speak my mind and secondly I do not compromise. I could have changed my career graph by becoming more adjusting and probably far more importantly by not voicing my views. Shri Girish Mehra the then Chief Secretary in 1984 recorded in my Annual Confidential Report (ACR) that she should exercise restraint of speech and Shri NK Sabharwal, the then Chairman of the State Textile Corporation recorded, "She will insist on her own point of view even when the majority of the senior officers hold an opinion different from hers." I would like to call a spade a spade. I see black and white, not shades of gray. I don't compromise. They could overrule me and give their orders in writing if they were so confident of their view and I would of course have no objection in carrying out the orders. But the problem arises when they want you to write their views as your own. These traits were neither appreciated then nor are they appreciated now. Much time is wasted in petty politics and ego issues. The perception outside about the Service is that the politicians and bureaucrats are involved in earth shaking decisions with far-reaching consequences, but you will be surprised to learn what petty issues preoccupy them and why decision-making is such a long and tedious job.

I could not conform to these expectations and consequently I was sidelined. Ministers and senior officers did not want me as their subordinate. My subordinates, I dare say, were mostly happy with me and would have found me very supportive. I have gone out of my way to stand by them and support them and take full responsibility for the decisions of the department.

Our youngsters must be clear before they decide to join the Civil Service, whether they want to enter the Service to make a difference or they want to join the Service for status, perks and power. They have to decide whether they are willing to make sacrifices in order to make a difference. We need youngsters who can stand up despite the reverses that they will be likely to suffer. Only that will put a stop to the deterioration all round.

This book has two parts. In first part I have narrated the problems I faced during my career and many of them were of a very petty nature. The second part is about the lessons I learnt and how in my view some of the problems faced by the country can be handled.

My father, Dr Jit Verma seeing his daughter going through myriad experiences had always stressed that I should keep a diary which of course I never did. He later on told me that if I had kept a diary, I could have written my memoirs. I thought to myself that I could still write from memory and that although notes would have helped, lack of them need not deter me. When suddenly placed under suspension by Ms Mayawati, I had a lot of time to remember the injustices done to me and consequently I began writing this book. My husband and my batchmate, P Uma Shankar was a great support. My daughter Tara Shankar Basu and my friend and batchmate from the Income Tax Service, Ms Shashi Kapila also provided their invaluable suggestions. Lastly, I must also thank Shri Rohit Kumar who took time out from his busy work schedule to help me put the book together. I thank them all profusely.

New Delhi

Promilla Shankar

Contents

PART I

PROBLEMS FACED

THIS PART brings out the inane trivialities, petty politics and corruption that is prevalent in UP. The system is not professional neither are the officers or the ministers. I want to tell the world outside who think of bureaucrats and ministers as being occupied with far reaching policy and implementation issues as to what really occupies their mind and how they function. I was shocked and so will the readers be that instead of thinking about serious developmental issues they are wasting their time on very petty issues. Neither do they work nor do they allow serious and dedicated officers to work towards improving the system. So when you join the service you must be prepared for what you will encounter.

The narration reveals how senior officers evade responsibility and try to implicate their junior officers, and how they attempt to sweep unpalatable issues under the carpet. They put up an artificial front that things are working smoothly and work of great import is being done very efficiently but if you just dig beneath the surface you will find rot underneath which nobody has the time or the inclination to rectify. If you go along, willing to play ball and agreeing to being exploited it is fine but if you do not acquiesce and have a different point of view you will not only not have a meteoric rise in your career but you will be harassed, transferred and more often than not lukewarm average entries if not adverse entries are awarded in your Annual Confidential Report.

All sectors of administration show the same rot that has set in including the police, the judiciary and the press. It is not merit that counts but connections in getting the so-called plum postings. Nepotism and favouritism flourish. Rules and regulations are openly defied and disregarded and if you want to go by the rule book you are put on the defensive and repeatedly called 'strict' and a 'stickler for rules'. You begin to wonder what rules are made for! I have written about the corruption that ministers indulge in. Not only do they not restrict themselves to big amounts but even very petty corruption is indulged in. There are caste lobbies which work in the interest of officers of the same caste, with the result that the so-called 'outsiders' do not have such an easy time. You are surprised because you are under the impression that caste equations would not matter among the so-called educated, elite group but you are surprised that even in the service caste equations count for a good deal. The functioning of the government as I experienced it in several departments of the government in UP will bring out succinctly the misgovernance and the corruption rampant in the State.

1

Additional City Magistrate, Kanpur

MY FIRST posting in July 1978 after the training period was to Kanpur. I was eager and looking forward to taking charge as a Sub-Divisional Magistrate, the first charge for any IAS officer. I reached Kanpur on 15th July 1978. The District Magistrate of Kanpur, Shri Kalyan Kumar Bakshi belonged to the 1964 batch of the IAS. Kanpur is an important city in UP. It was considered a prestigious posting for a District Magistrate, in the same league as being posted to Lucknow, Allahabad, Varanasi and Agra. These five districts were together known as KAVAL towns. Only officers who had done a couple of smaller districts were posted to these bigger districts. These districts were also sensitive from the point of view of law and order and so besides Sub-Division Magistrates they also had posts of City Magistrates, whose basic work was to ensure the law and order in their areas.

I reached the District Magistrate's office straight from the railway station and introduced myself. After some cursory talk I asked Shri Bakshi about the arrangements for my stay in Kanpur. He informed me that I was to stay with him and his family in the DM's house. Mrs Bakshi had already got a room prepared for me. Such consideration for a junior colleague, now non-existent, was rare even in those days. For more than a month I continued to stay with them. I can never forget their kindness. Mrs Bakshi would herself bring me a cup of tea in the morning, embarrassing me no end. I was at that time extremely shy and consequently did not feel totally at home. After all Mr Bakshi was my boss and I was a little constrained at having to be on my best behaviour at all times. After persistent persuasion Mr Bakshi finally allotted me a one bed room set in the officer's hostel and I set-up my own place.

People like the Bakshis were not to be found in the service as I was going to find soon thereafter. I am narrating this because taking care and guiding young officers was rare. The once existing tradition of the ICS/IAS where the youngsters were considered a part of the family was long over. I soon realized that it was my good fortune that I started my first posting after the mandatory two year probationary period with Mr Bakshi.

IAS officers after their two years training are normally posted as Sub-Divisional Magistrates in the district which is under the District Magistrate. The district, is divided into three, four or more Sub-Divisions or Tehsils depending upon the size of the district. Each Sub-Division is under the control of a Sub-Divisional Officer who is responsible for revenue collection, implementation of the government's schemes pertaining to development, maintaining the law and order situation in his Sub-Division and also holding court to decide revenue cases. As mentioned earlier, bigger towns with large urban areas also had City Magistrates.

Mr Bakshi took upon himself the onus of training further a fresh officer and pointing out the pitfalls young and inexperienced officers face when they actually embark on their careers. He would tell me about his own times when he had joined service and the problems he had faced. I was soon going to rue the day when shortly thereafter Mr Bakshi was transferred to the Home Department in Lucknow and he was succeeded by a State Civil Service officer promoted to the IAS, Shri Munni Lal. Mr Bakshi had posted me as an 'Additional City Magistrate' and my jurisdiction extended to the police stations of Babupurwa, Govindnagar and Juhi. I was to be responsible for the law and order situation in this area and the hierarchy above me for this purpose was the City Magistrate, the Additional District Magistrate (City) and finally the DM.

My area of jurisdiction had two major institutions, the Nirankari Bhawan and the DAV College. Law and order in these two institutions proved to be a source of great anxiety and endless trouble. The Deputy Superintendent of Police Shri Dharam Singh, who was my counterpart in the police to look after the law and order situation, was an elderly gentleman from the provincial police service, just a few years from retirement. The magistrates and the police officers have to work in tandem for handling law and order problems as the police normally requires the orders of a magistrate to use force to disperse mobs and control a violent situation.

One morning I reached the Collectorate and on the spur of the moment decided to check the attendance at the

Revenue Record Room which was also under my charge. I completed my surprise inspection and reached my office at about 11 o'clock when I heard a rumour about police firing in the Nirankari Bhawan at Babupurwa. Since that was in my area of jurisdiction, I immediately tried to contact the City Magistrate and the Additional District Magistrate (City) who were in overall control of the law and order situation in the city. These officers were not present in their offices and I was told that they were on around of the city. Their staff was non-committal. It is customary in UP that the staff will not tell you the boss's whereabouts. The standard reply is he is out, we don't know where he is or when he will return. I could not contact my police counterpart either and so decided to go to Babupurwa myself. I would like to mention here that there were no mobile telephones those days and the landline telephone system was far from efficient.

The Nirankari Bhawan was a bloody sight. The trouble seemed to have taken place quite early. The Nirankari Baba had come to Kanpur to give discourses, much to the chagrin of the Akalis. Early that morning the Akalis attacked the Bhawan, slaughtering men, women and children. There were blood stains on the walls, floors and the staircase. It was an emergency which we in the district administration had failed to anticipate. When they heard about the trouble the District Magistrate's office had immediately contacted the Deputy Superintendent of Police who probably had no time to inform me or take me along. He rushed to the spot, where to control the situation the police had to resort to firing. Unfortunately thirteen people died that morning. It was a big tragedy for Kanpur, the like of which it had not seen.

The Nirankaris soon after the tragedy began to insist on taking the bodies in a public procession for the funeral. They would not listen to reason. After much deliberation, the district administration, at the highest level, bowed to the demand, in spite of the great risks involved. All the officers were present at the spot that evening including the District Magistrate and the Senior Superintendent of Police. I and the Deputy Superintendent of Police were to accompany the procession in one jeep. It was an explosive situation. It was evening time and getting dark. I can never forget the palpable tension that prevailed as we accompanied the procession. There were massive crowds that had poured out onto the roads. They were in a state of emotional frenzy shouting slogans at the top of their voices. The rooftops too were crowded with onlookers. At one point the electricity failed, giving rise to panic. The thought of what could have happened was extremely sobering. I was extremely aware about my inexperience. Luckily the funeral procession went off without any incident.

For the next couple of weeks, I and the Deputy Superintendent of Police would spend our entire day at the Nirankari Bhawan to ensure that nothing untoward happened. This time the Deputy Superintendent of Police would call at my residence and we would go to the spot together.

There was a huge hue and cry in the city subsequently. The district administration came in for a lot of criticism for not being able to avert the tragedy. As was expected, a judicial enquiry was finally instituted in the matter under the chairmanship of Shri Ashwini Kumar a retired IAS officer, to fix responsibility. The very next day, early in the morning at about 8 o'clock, Shri Bakshi, who was now Special Secretary, Home Department paid me a visit from Lucknow. He was extremely upset and had come to warn me to be very careful. He felt that Shri Munni Lal and the Additional District Magistrate (City) Shri CS Dwivedi in their efforts at evading responsibility would try to implicate me, I being the junior most officer in the chain. Shri Bakshi told me to mention clearly the date and time on all communications received by me because he felt that the senior officers would try to cover their tracks by issuing back dated orders. I was a little disbelieving and felt that perhaps in his concern for me Shri Bakshi was overreacting. But his fears were not misplaced as I was to find soon thereafter.

Soon enough I began to get letters from Shri Munni Lal, District Magistrate and Shri CS Dwivedi, the Additional District Magistrate (City) calling for my explanation as to why I had not reached the Nirankari Bhawan on time. The entire episode was a major failure on the part of the intelligence authorities and also on the part of the Additional District Magistrate (City) who failed to issue the requisite advisories to the officers. It was indeed a tough situation for a young officer where on the one hand you did not have the experience and on the other hand you were unable to trust the senior officers and had to remain alert and suspicious of them all the time. To make my position clear and to prove that I was in office and not absconding, I submitted my reply along with a photocopy of my inspection note of the Revenue Record Room. I had to do this post haste, as I was warned that these papers of the revenue record room could easily be made to disappear. I hired a locker to keep copies of documents I had submitted as again I was warned that the attachments of my reply could also be made to vanish. Not playing ball and not going along with the district administration, however, earned me the antagonism of the District Magistrate and the Additional District Magistrate (City).

I was finally not summoned by the enquiry commission looking to my reply. The enquiry went on for some time causing a lot of stress and anxiety, so much that my counterpart the Deputy Superintendent of Police Shri Dharam Singh soon died of a heart attack.

The other institution which gave me trouble during my stint in Kanpur was the DAV College. It was notorious for unions and student problems and trouble was always brewing there. Examinations approached and I and the Deputy Superintendent of Police were given orders to be physically present in the college and make it our headquarters till such time as the examinations ended. I and the Deputy Superintendent of Police would leave early in the morning and stay in the college till late afternoon. Things went on smoothly for a few days but then the students went on rampage in protest against the checks in the college to curb cheating. Things came to a head when some students were caught red-handed.

The student agitation went on for several days at the college gates. They would raise slogans and sit on dharna, all because they were not allowed to cheat! As a section was also preventing other students from entering and sitting for the exam, we ensured that they were not allowed to succeed. Their angst then diverted itself against the police. One day the students marched to the police station and began shouting slogans at the gates. We shut the gates and barricaded them. We tried to get in touch with the District Magistrate, the Additional District Magistrate (City) and their Police counterparts but to no avail. We had to inform them about the situation and also that we were in dire need of police reinforcements. Wireless messages were sent. We were informed that the messages have been relayed and that these officers were on their way. The students were getting unruly, their strength kept on increasing and they refused to listen to reason. They began climbing the gates and also began breaking the wall of the police station. Things were going out of hand. The abuses hurled by the students were making the constables very angry. The Deputy Superintendent of Police asked me a couple of times whether we could use force. As has been mentioned earlier, police needs the orders of a Magistrate to use force. There was no alternative but to give permission. I gave permission for lathi charge and the constables with their lathis swooped down on the students with war cries. Tear gas shells were also fired. There were shrieks and stampedes and utter chaos. I had not seen anything like this before. However, the situation could soon be brought under control. The mobs were dispersed. After the situation got under control, we could see brick bats scattered as far away as half-a-kilometre. Senior officers and police reinforcements as always, arrived after the battle was over. The higher echelons leave you to fend for yourself and try and evade responsibility. This is a lesson you learn early in you career.

Half-a-dozen students had suffered fractures while the others got away with minor injuries. A student leader was one of those who was more seriously injured including a broken leg. He had to spend some time in jail too. Many years later sometime in the '90s he came to see me. He told me that because of this incident and the thrashing that he had received (courtesy me!) had paved the way for his entry into politics and he was now a Member of the Legislative Assembly (MLA).

These incidents during my very first posting after probation made me realize that you are on your own. Nobody helps you and neither can you depend on anyone. You have to fend for yourself even if you are totally raw and inexperienced. Your senior officers, who are expected to guide and support you, will probably try to implicate you to save themselves. You have to be on your guard. Your seniors will not support you and you cannot trust them.

2

Additional District Magistrate (Project), Meerut

THE POLICY of the government is that wherever possible husband and wife should be posted at the same place. Shortly after getting married in March 1979, I and my husband P Uma Shankar were posted to district Meerut in Western UP as Additional District Magistrates. I was to take over charge as Additional District Magistrate (Project) and Project Director SFDA and IRDP and my husband was to take over as Additional District Magistrate (Development). Our boss was the District Magistrate Shri AP Singh of the 1967 batch of the IAS.

We took over our respective jobs in the summer of 1979. As Additional District Magistrate (Project) my job involved the implementation of the SFDA and IRDP projects. SFDA and IRDP were related to the small and marginal farmers' development. The purpose of these programmes was to supply adequate subsidized credit to small and marginal farmers as well as agricultural labour so that they could adopt the latest techniques of cultivation as well as diversify their activities by undertaking dairy, poultry, piggery, horticulture and other activities. The major programmes included credit for buying buffaloes and bullock carts. It was projected that these income earning assets would help them cross the poverty line. These schemes meant the flow of large amounts of credit from banks for the purchase of buffaloes, bullock carts etc. Thus it could be seen as an important assignment for extending patronage. At a time when resources were scarce, the attraction of an agency flush with funds and mandated to spend the same through procurement could well be understood. The agency was also not dependent on typical financial rules for drawing funds from the treasury, as the funds were released by the Government of India also directly to the Agency's bank account.

The post of Additional District Magistrate (Project) had been lying vacant for some time and the work was being looked after by the then Additional District Magistrate (Development) as an additional charge. As he had his hands full with his own job, he rarely came to the office of the Additional District Magistrate (Project). Under the circumstances the Additional Project Director had virtually a free hand and was functioning as the *de facto* Project Director. He was using the official vehicle of the Project Director as well as the latter's residential telephone. It is important to mention here that, he, the Additional Projector Director, was the nephew of the then Chief Minister of UP, Shri Banarsi Das. The above arrangement presumably suited the District Magistrate and when I joined as Project Director he expected that I would allow this to continue.

I took charge of my office and in due course a house was allotted to me. I took control of my official vehicle and had my residential telephone installed at my camp office. The office at the residence of an officer is generally known as the camp office. While I was in the process of settling down, I realized that the District Magistrate Shri AP Singh seemed annoyed with me. This upset me a little as one is ever keen to keep the boss happy so that he grades you as an outstanding officer when he assesses your capabilities and achievements for the annual report and so I approached Shri AP Singh to find out what the problem was. He burst out saying that you have taken away 'his' vehicle and 'his' telephone. It took me sometime to understand what he was alluding to. I was shocked, to say the least. I had to tell him that I could not treat my subordinate as my boss even if he happened to be the Chief Minister's nephew. I had only taken what was officially mine.

In retrospect, I would think that the District Magistrate would have expected me to continue to function as nominal Project Director, allowing the Additional Project Director to have full sway over the activities of the agency. My taking the official car and the telephone, though small in themselves, would have been interpreted by the District Magistrate as my unwillingness to conform. The Additional Project Director being the Chief Minister's nephew, the desire of the District Magistrate to please the Additional Project Director and thereby please the Chief Minister could be well understood.

This was the beginning of a very unpleasant relationship with Shri AP Singh. He soon began to find fault with everything I did. The District Magistrate could not have directly told me to allow the Additional Project Director to function freely. Therefore he resorted to harassing me by finding fault with everything I did and by setting unrealistic timelines and by humiliating me. He would ring up the office at 10 o'clock sharp to check whether I was in office in time or not. He would ring up in the afternoon to check whether I had gone home for lunch and how much time I took over it. He began to create all sorts of problems for me. I had in the course of my work blacklisted a couple of manufacturers of bullock carts. This also annoyed him. I was holding a meeting of the Block Development Officers, when he rang me up and kept up a one sided tirade. I could not respond to him as I was in the midst of a meeting and did not want to let the officers in the meeting in on what was happening but my expression must have shown that something was drastically wrong.

I was also at the time in the family way and as my job entailed quite a bit of travel and touring, my doctor had advised me that for some time I should refrain from travelling on bumpy roads. I thought it prudent to inform the DM before he got further annoyed and charged me with dereliction of duty. It was in keeping with Shri AP Singh's character that exactly two days later he summoned me to his office and gave me a complaint about the supply of defective PVC pipes and asked me to submit a report by that same evening. This enquiry could have been done by any other officer. It did not pertain to my project. The enquiry involved a visit to a far away block but as I expected to be back by lunch time, I left straightaway from his office without informing anyone. I was in for a rude shock. On reaching the block office I was told that the supplies were at several sites in the interior. Moreover there were no roads, only kuchcha bumpy paths. The whole day I was on these dusty paths and could come back to Meerut quite late at night. Those were the times when there were no mobile telephones. From the villages in the interior I could not inform anyone about my whereabouts. My husband was in a frenzy, wondering what had happened to me. It was lucky that I escaped any serious mishap that day. Having by now seen through the DM's sinister intentions, I made up my mind that I will henceforth not allow him to be that inconsiderate.

The situation gradually kept worsening. Shri AP Singh's attitude became very humiliating. He was unhappy that we did not invite him for dinners. We had just joined service. We had no infrastructure at that time, not even a fridge. A writing table was doubling up as a dining table. We were not equipped for social entertaining. He would openly crib about it and also mention that they take away two-two salaries as if it was a fault that we were a working couple. The pettiness and small mindedness of this man was unbelievable.

Time soon came for my confinement and I proceeded on leave to Delhi to be with my parents. The charge of my post was given to another officer. Lady officers according to government rules at that time were entitled only for three months maternity leave. At about the time my leave was getting exhausted, my husband informed me that the District Magistrate wanted me to extend my leave. He told me that the District Magistrate over the past sometime had been repeatedly telling him that he should tell me to extend my leave and also that he would ensure that the Chief Medical Officer of the district would complete all the necessary formalities and give the requisite medical certificate. Under normal circumstances I would have extended my leave but this put my back up and I decided that I would rejoin immediately on expiry of three months. Leaving my son Rohit with my mother, I reached Meerut and went to meet the District Magistrate Shri AP Singh. For a change he seemed quite cheerful and cordial. He offered me a cup of tea. After the niceties, he asked me whether I was ready for my appointment with the Chief Medical Officer. When I informed him that I had come to give my joining report his face fell and his entire demeanour changed. He told the officer who was holding additional charge of my post not to handover charge to me. He kept me on compulsory wait for a month before the Appointments Department of the government at Lucknow which is in-charge of postings and transfers, once again issued orders and a directive to Shri AP Singh to allow me to rejoin my old post of Additional District Magistrate (Project) on return from maternity leave. I showed this order to the District Magistrate and proceeded to take charge of my office. This was indeed a slap on the face of Shri AP Singh and the relationship after this was irretrievably damaged.

It was now the end of February and the financial year was coming to a close. I had to work extremely hard to achieve the targets. Loaning for various component schemes had to be finalized and disbursed with the approval of the District Magistrate. The District Magistrate was undermining my performance by delaying approvals. Cheques which were submitted to the District Magistrate for counter signatures kept lying in his office for long periods, leading to delay in disbursements. The accountants who took the files to him for his signatures were returned with one excuse or another. I had to then take the files personally to ensure that he signed and did not keep them pending with one excuse or another. I was also quite sure that he wanted me to perform poorly so that he could write in my Annual Confidential Report that targets had not been achieved.

The District Magistrate was also trying to get me shifted out and he finally succeeded. Towards the end of April 1980, I was posted as Staff Officer to the Commissioner of Meerut Division, Shri RK Dhar and subsequently Shri RD Sonker. The District Magistrate Shri AP Singh gave me an adverse report which was repudiated by both the Commissioner of Meerut Division as the Reviewing Officer and the Agricultural Production Commissioner in Lucknow as the Accepting Officer. Those days adverse entries to young officers were unheard of. The IAS cadre was shocked and many officers were sympathetic.

Shri AP Singh warped the entire working environment. Instead of giving our whole-hearted attention to the job at hand I found myself preoccupied with the unnecessary tension created by him. He was a male chauvinist who was strongly biased against women. Voted some years later by the UP IAS Officers Association as the most corrupt officer of UP, Shri AP Singh had started on this track rather early in his career. Power had obviously gone to his head and he felt that whatever he said was law. He broke all rules and regulations and expected others to toe his line. He was one of a few of this kind then. Unfortunately things in UP have changed dramatically and there are very many officers like him today.

3

Joint Commissioner (Ramganga Command Area Development Project), Kanpur

THE POSTING in Meerut was followed by that in Lucknow as Deputy Secretary, Housing Department and subsequently as Under Secretary in the Home Department in Government of India. When we reverted back to UP we thought that with the addition of our second child Tara we might be better able to handle both home and office there due to the slightly better infrastructural support, proximity of office to home and better availability of domestic staff in a smaller town. We reached Kanpur once again. I was posted as Joint Administrator of the Ramganga Command Area Development Project. The Administrator was Shri Devi Dayal of the 1966 batch of the IAS.

Command Area Projects had been set-up in UP in the catchment areas of the rivers Ramganga, Sharda and Gandak, basically to improve the availability and the optimum utilization of these river waters for irrigation. There were thus three command area development projects in UP at that time. The primary objective of the Command Area Development Projects was to bridge the gap between the irrigation potential created and its utilization through the development of field channels, drains, reclamation of water logged areas, enforcement of a proper system of warabandi (system of water distribution and supply schedule), provision of inputs for agriculture, horticulture and so on.

I enjoyed travelling around the Command Area which stretched from Mathura through Agra to Kanpur. Shri Devi Dayal was a very active, enthusiastic and indefatigable man. I learnt a lot from him. However it was unfortunate that shortly afterwards Shri Devi Dayal was transferred out and the additional charge of this post was given to Shri AP Singh about whom I have already written in the preceding chapter. Shri AP Singh who was then working as Commissioner of the Allahabad Division was given additional charge of the post of Administrator of the Ramganga Command Area Development Project till such time as a regular posting was made.

The situation henceforth was not destined to be normal. This was the year 1984. Shri AP Singh had by then gained a reputation for corruption. Within a week of his taking over additional charge he sent me a note, asking that a payment of ₹ 2 lakh be made to a firm of architects whom he was thinking of entrusting with the task of taking up a project for the construction of the office building of the Ramganga Project. There was no file, no proper noting except these few lines written on a piece of paper. Everybody knows that money in a government office is not doled out like this. There was no proposal for the construction of the office building nor had it been placed before the Board at any time. Only after the Boards approval and the government's clearance could such a proposal be taken forward. Moreover the selection of the architect too has to follow laid down procedures. So I wrote back to him that it was not clear as to when the scheme for construction of the office building for the Ramganga Command Area was approved and how the architects had been selected. After this episode he again embarked on his old practice of asking for my explanation on all and sundry matters. The entire office was soon aware of the bad relations between the Administrator and the Joint Administrator. The only saving grace was that I did not have to confront him on a daily basis. As he was based in Allahabad, he would come to Kanpur about twice a week.

On first hearing of the orders giving Shri AP Singh the additional charge of the Ramganga Command Area Project, I had made up my mind that I will not allow the history of bad relations with him in my earlier posting to affect my present functioning. However, this was not to be and therefore I decided that I would not work with him for more than three months. Working for a period beyond three months entitles your superior to write your Confidential Report. I did not welcome the prospect of representing against an adverse report once again.

There was an exchange of bitter correspondence with him. He started sending me letters every day making all sorts of allegations and finding shortcomings. I would find three or four letters together in an envelope. I had no option but to reply in self-defence because otherwise it would be assumed that I had nothing to say against his charges. I was interested that either Shri AP Singh or I should be shifted out. It was not possible for us to work together. I met the Agricultural Production Commissioner Shri Kalyana Krishnan, a very fine officer of the 1955 batch. Shri Kalyana Krishnan too was a source of great strength to me and very supportive. He was totally unflappable and made my problems seem nothing at all. In the meantime my efforts at getting a change of job bore fruit and I was told that orders for shifting me to the Directorate of Labour in Kanpur itself were being issued. However even before a copy of the orders could reach me, Shri AP Singh relieved me in absentia on 23 January 1985. It was another matter that the person whom I was to relieve in the Directorate of Labour managed to get his transfer stayed and I found myself in a situation where I was unable to join my new place of posting and also at the same time stood relieved from my present job. Thus, I remained on compulsory wait for about two weeks, after which I was posted as Managing Director of the UP State Spinning Mills Company No 1 again at Kanpur.

The interesting part about this episode is that while waiting for a posting, I had gone to Lucknow to meet the Chief Secretary to apprise him of the situation and also to ask him for a posting in Kanpur itself where my husband too was posted as the Administrator of the Kanpur Municipal Corporation. The Chief Secretary was Shri Girish Mehra of the 1954 batch. I had just about introduced myself when

Shri Mehra erupted with great vehemence. He was extremely harsh and rude and took me to task for writing the letters that I had written to Shri AP Singh. It was obvious that Shri AP Singh had already briefed him his side of the story. However, I told Shri Mehra that I had only responded to the letters written by Shri AP Singh as I had no option but to respond to his letters in self-defence. But I found that Shri Mehra was already prejudiced and unwilling to listen to me. His strategy was to take a very aggressive stand and cower me into submission. I was shocked by his belligerence but maintained that it was not my fault. I ensured thereafter that I never came face to face with him, taking every precaution to not cross his path. His totally one sided and prejudiced attitude was unforgivable from the head of the State Administration.

A year or two later, I opened a letter from the Appointments Department communicating to me that Shri Mehra as Chief Secretary had given me some adverse remarks which however were not being treated by the department as adverse but more so in the nature of advice. They left the option to me whether I wanted to challenge and have them deleted or let them be. Shri Mehra had made remarks to the effect that I should exercise restraint of speech etc. I let this pass as I could not muster the energy to get involved with one more representation. Preparing such a representation means that one has to spend a lot of time on unnecessary and unfruitful work and relive episodes you would rather forget. It brought home to me that things are not fair. Here was a man who refused to even give me a chance to explain my version and kept on a one sided tirade. He could not tolerate a junior officer speaking up. It is a fact that most officers like submissive yes men and yes women.

In the initial few years of my service, I already had two adverse reports and Shri Munni Lal too would have, I presume, given me a very mediocre report. All this, not for any lack of commitment and performance but for extraneous considerations as is very often the case.

4

Managing Director (UP State Spinning Mills Company No 1), Kanpur

MY POSTING as Joint Administrator Ramganga Command Area Development Project was followed as Managing Director of the UP State Spinning Mills Company No 1 in Kanpur itself. The State Textile Corporation was the holding company with an installed capacity of 2.5 lakh spindles. It had two subsidiaries, Company No 1 with a capacity of 2 lakh spindles and Company No 2 with a capacity of 1 lakh spindles. There was also a Cooperative Spinning Federation with a sizable capacity. All these four companies besides their Managing Directors, had a common full time Chairman. The Chairman at that time was Shri M Varadarajan (1956 batch), but was soon followed by Shri NK Sabharwal of the 1965 batch.

I took over as Managing Director of the UP State Spinning Mills Company No 1 in February 1985. The company comprised of four mills of 50,000 spindles each, located at Rae

Bareli, Maunath Bhanjan, Barabanki and Akbarpur. It had a turnover of ₹ 60 crore at that time. The job entailed buying cotton, manufacturing yarn and marketing the yarn.

The year 1985 was not a good one for the spinning sector and all the mills barring a few were making losses. The mills were facing serious labour problems and indiscipline and had huge unsold inventories of yarn. It was felt that the indiscriminate expansion of the installed capacity was the major reason for the difficulties being faced by the mills. Although the mills were initially making reasonable profits, the management under the chairmanship of Shri Prabhat Kumar of the 1961 batch had decided to double their installed capacity. The general belief in the organisation was that this doubling of the installed capacity of spindles perhaps without proper assessment of economic viability saw their steep decline into loss making mills.

This job as Managing Director of the Spinning Company required commercial expertise, as the prices of cotton and yarn are in a continuous state of flux due to market forces. The price could fluctuate several times a day. Although there were senior managers to advice you on these matters, one was generally hesitant about taking decisions on buying and selling because of lack of knowledge and also because you knew that your managers could not be trusted implicitly. You however had no option but to go by the advice of your manager and hope for the best. Technical parameters of the mills aside, I felt that buying cotton at the lowest price and selling yarn at the highest price possible, given the circumstances at any time was the main area where profits of the company could be maximized. I doubt if any of the

Managing Directors who all belonged to the IAS was able to play this role effectively for lack of knowledge and expertise in these commercial operations.

I presumed that it was because of this lack of knowledge and to evade responsibility that the STC group had evolved a very strange system of management which was in operation. The companies had resorted to what was called joint decision making. The cotton purchase committees included all the Managers (Purchase), the financial controllers, the joint managing directors as well as the Managing Directors of all the four companies. Likewise the yarn selling committees included all the above but instead of Managers (Purchase) the Managers (Marketing) were included. If any of these managers heard of any development, a meeting would be called at short notice. The stock of inventory would be taken and the yarn rates would be decided based on the inputs in the meeting. Sometimes there would be bitter arguments between the marketing managers of the various companies who wanted the rates to be fixed depending on their individual inventories and problems but the standard practice was to fix the same rates for all. Your marketing manager would instigate you that rates were being fixed keeping in mind the interest of the holding company and all this created a lot of bad blood.

The matter of allowing companies to take their own decisions on trading was taken up several times with the Chairman Shri NK Sabharwal but the matter could never be finalized. I might mention here that fixing the rates of yarn was a very complex issue as there were many types of yarn being produced. We were manufacturing about 30-40 yarns of different counts both in cone and hank. The whole exercise of fixing prices was a real farce. The Managing Directors went by the advice of their Marketing Managers for wont of expert knowledge and remained more or less silent spectators. Very often we heard whispers about corruption and the vested interests of the Marketing Managers.

The technical parameters of my mills improved. Capacity utilization increased. The labour situation was tackled head on. I ensured that we followed the principle of no work no pay. The mill at Akbarpur was particularly troublesome although it had the best machinery. I was lucky that for a while there was no Chairman as Shri Varadarajan of the 1956 batch had been transferred and Shri NK Sabharwal had not yet joined. This was a lucky break, as otherwise there would have been a lot of pressure to settle labour disputes at the earliest. This was a tug of war in which we held out and when the unions realized that the management was not willing to compromise on unreasonable demands and meant business they behaved. However, as far as buying and selling of the cotton and yarn was concerned one remained on a weak footing. Moreover in view of the system of management prevailing there was nothing much that one could do.

I worked as Managing Director of the UP State Spinning Mills Company No 1 for two years. At the beginning of 1987, one of our dealers absconded with yarn worth ₹ 60 lakh without retiring the documents and was unable to pay up. This took place with the connivance of the Marketing Manager, one Shri Rizvi. When I brought this matter to the notice of the Chairman, Shri Sabharwal was insistent that we should keep this matter to ourselves and not publicize it.

However, when all our efforts for getting the money back failed, I informed the Chairman that not only was an FIR required to be lodged against the transporter and the dealer but action would also have to be taken against the Marketing Manager. However, the Chairman would not agree and the whole system of joint decision making sprang into operation to pressurize me.

The Chairman would hold meetings of all the Managing Directors and the Joint Managing Directors to dissuade me from proposing my course of action. Incidentally, I would like to mention here that the Chairman was close to the Manager Marketing of my company. The Chairman had taken over the entire work relating to export of yarn of all the companies and made Shri Rizvi the coordinator. This Manager Marketing had accompanied the Chairman on his foreign tours in connection with the exports and was very close to him. Shri Rizvi had the audacity to put up a proposal in the committee that the transporter was willing to get deducted a small amount of money on every truck of yarn that he lifted for us. This in effect meant that we were bound to give him the contract of our transportation for years to come. On one hand he had caused massive loss to us, on the other hand we were required to give him the transport business in perpetuity, whereas the procedure was to call for bids every year. I told the Chairman that this was unthinkable. When I realized that the Chairman was tying my hands from all sides and did not seem amenable to any of my suggestions, I sent him my proposal in writing recorded on the file for his approval. Shri Sabharwal called me to his room the next day. He was furious and threw the file at me. I thought this reason enough to proceed on leave but the financial year was coming to an end so I thought that that would not be the right time to proceed on leave. I waited for the end of the financial year so that the accounts could be finalized. I also finalized the enquiry report against the Manager Marketing and finally from 1 April 1987 I proceeded on leave. Shri Sabharwal was now desperate because the onus would fall on him and he would himself be liable to take a decision in the matter. He requested the Chief Secretary to cancel my leave and spoke to me also to return but I told him that it was not possible for me to function in the prevalent atmosphere.

Shri Sabharwal had given me a very good report in the preceding year but suddenly at the end of the financial year 1987 he changed his mind. One of the things he said was that she holds her own even when the majority opinion of senior officers is against her. I did happen to be the junior most officer in that set-up which I found very disadvantageous. The Managing Director of the Cooperative Federation, Shri Nagendra Singh belonged to the 1968 batch, the Managing Director of the State Textile Corporation, Shri Vinod Malhotra belonged to the 1971 batch and that of the UP State Spinning Mills Company No 2, Shri NA Vishwanathan belonged to the 1972 batch. I from the 1976 batch was of course the junior most. As this episode related to my company I was primarily responsible for it. I did not see why I should compromise on principles of fair play and just retribution, to bail out somebody. The Chairman was neither willing to take action against the transporter nor against the Marketing Manager. He wanted that the situation just be swept under the carpet. He did not want that any adverse situation should get highlighted during his tenure.

As a matter of policy, I feel that the government should not get into commercial operations. It is not the job of the government. Additionally such jobs require a degree of technical expertise which most officers of the IAS will not have. Moreover, a lot of time is spent in hushing up things and sweeping them under the carpet instead of taking them head on and handling them as they should be handled. Taking the right decision does not take time but when vested interests get involved, a lot of time and energy is wasted.

5

Joint Development Commissioner, Jhansi

WHILE I was holding office as Managing Director of the UP State Spinning Mills Company No 1, my husband was the District Magistrate in the adjoining district of Fatehpur. It was approximately 80 kms from Kanpur. After taking leave I joined him in Fatehpur with the children, hoping soon for a joint posting thereafter. Finally we did get one. My husband was posted as District Magistrate Jhansi and I joined as the Joint Development Commissioner of Jhansi Division.

Jhansi Division comprised the districts of Jhansi, Lalitpur, Hamirpur, Jalaun and Banda. This area is also known as Bundelkhand. As this division was quite backward, it was not a posting which made the officers very happy. Not many officers in UP were willing to go to Bundelkhand, to the hills or to Eastern UP. I feel, however that Bundelkhand is beautiful with several beautiful sites and dams and is also resonant with history. There are the forts of Jhansi which incidentally could be seen on the hillock from our residence (DM's residence), Kalpi, etc. The forts and temples of Orchha and the temples of Khajuraho in Madhya Pradesh are not too far away. This area also is sparsely populated as compared to other regions of UP and in 1987 you could drive for more than 50 kms without seeing anyone. This was one posting that I really enjoyed and I loved to go on tours into the interiors.

There was a total overhaul of the bureaucracy in Jhansi and it so happened by a quirky coincidence that the Commissioner, the Joint Development Commissioner, the District Magistrate and the Superintendent of Police all joined Jhansi on the same day, ie 22nd July 1987. The Commissioner our boss Shri Babu Ram belonged to the 1968 batch of the IAS.

All of us reached Jhansi in the midst of a crisis. The summer of 1987 was extremely bad for Bundelkhand. The monsoon had failed and there was a massive drought. As soon as we took charge in the district we got busy with handling the drought situation. Extensive travelling was required to assess the situation. Arrangements had to be made immediately even for alternative sources of drinking water, let alone irrigation facilities, fodder for cattle, supply of seeds, waiving of farmers loans and so on. I toured very extensively all through the division including also the 'Patha' area of Banda District, a hilly ragged terrain, notorious for dacoits. Rains however did arrive but much later towards the end of September and thankfully the worst was over.

Shri Babu Ram, the Commissioner, would take monthly

meetings of the District Magistrates of the five districts under his jurisdiction to review the law and order situation and the rural development works in the districts. He made it a point to pick on one of the District Magistrates for 'special' treatment in every meeting. He had a habit of writing nasty letters to all the District Magistrates and his practice was to keep a file on each District Magistrate and other officers under him. The District Magistrates were most unhappy with him. Initially a couple of them tried to speak to him about it, but in vain. I even saw one lady District Magistrate weeping in front of him. He did not treat the officers well and would grill them and humiliate them in front of their junior officers.

I escaped this facet of his personality in the initial months as I was a part of his office to help him in his developmental duties in the division. I would apprise him every couple of days about the developments in the division. Monitoring the activities in the division, I found that a few Block Development Officers were particularly lagging behind and not performing even after repeated warnings. One such Block Development Officer by name Ahirwar was particularly bad and guilty also of corrupt practices. I spoke to the Commissioner about taking action against him. I told him that we required to take some action and that I would be sending him a file to charge-sheet and suspend one of the Block Development Officers. The Commissioner was quite enthusiastic that action was being proposed to punish a non-performing and corrupt Block Development Officer and felt that it would serve as a warning to the others also. He agreed with my suggestion and said that he would approve the suspension. When I sent the file to the Commissioner I found that it did not return with his approval for quite some time. On reminding the Commissioner about it he sent the file back to me with orders to discuss the matter. I went to discuss the issue with him but found that we discussed all matters irrelevant and inane but this particular file could not be discussed. He fixed another date for discussing the same. Finally he sent the file back to me with a series of queries. Discussing the matter with my staff and the inordinate delay in getting this file cleared, I was told that Shri Babu Ram will not clear the matter and sanction action against the Block Development Officer because he belonged to the same caste as the Commissioner, Shri Babu Ram.

This was my first brush with caste politics. I had had a very cosmopolitan upbringing having been educated in convent schools in the metro cities of Delhi, Mumbai and Chennai. One was hardly aware of caste issues and neither did one ever discuss them. In fact, whenever there was any vacancy and the need arose for recruitment, I would reduce the number of applicants by saying that we would recruit only a person from the Scheduled Caste. Shri Babu Ram's behaviour however made one conscious of the caste factor for the first time. Things began to fall into place. I could now understand why he was so rough and rude to Shri Pandey, District Magistrate of Banda. The reasons for his attitude over the last several months became clear and put one's back up.

The Scheduled Caste officers those days had formed a party called the DS4, which had I was told district as well as divisional units. They held regular weekly meetings. The Chairman of the meeting would be chosen by rotation irrespective of his seniority and the junior most Scheduled Caste functionary could also be the Chairman at some meeting. He would then occupy the chair of the Commissioner as these meeting were held after office hours in the Commissioner's office and the Commissioner would sit in front of him. These meetings were held behind closed doors and kept secret. I found that each Scheduled Caste officer would go all out to support another person belonging to the Scheduled Caste irrespective of the merits of the case. Caught on the wrong foot and unable to defend his position Shri Babu Ram started creating problems for me too, after this episode. Our relationship deteriorated. He kept asking for the file but I locked it up in my almirah fearing that if I sent it to him again he might destroy the file altogether.

The relationship of the Commissioner with all the five District Magistrates and the Joint Development Commissioner was severely strained. Work began to suffer. Some of the District Magistrates informed the Chief Secretary about the situation and sought transfers. Finally, Shri Babu Ram was transferred from Jhansi and replaced by Smt Sumita Kandpal of 1965 batch which saw things finally return to normalcy in the Division.

The Babu Ram episode made me conscious of the caste factor for the first time. I began to notice the aggressiveness of the Scheduled Caste officers. The matter that I had put up for Shri Babu Ram's sanction was genuine and was not motivated by any consideration other than official merit. I was not aware about the Block Development Officer's caste or creed nor had I heard the name Ahirwar before my posting in Jhansi. But the deep seated hatred that Shri Babu Ram nurtured for the upper castes and which created so much trouble for the officers was quite unnerving. Such attitudes not only vitiate the atmosphere but hamper the work. They create mistrust and do nothing to improve caste equations, but only make them worse.

6

Director (ICDS), Lucknow

FROM JHANSI I and my husband moved to Lucknow. He left Jhansi in June 1989 and I left in September 1989. Shri Shaibal Mukherjee of the 1965 batch was Secretary of the Social Welfare Department and wanted me to join his department as Director of the Integrated Child Development Scheme (ICDS). Things in the ICDS were not too good and I was not at all keen to join that department. The then incumbent on the post Smt Jayati Chandra of the 1975 batch, was having serious difficulties there due to the rampant corruption and vested interests in the department. There had also been a firing during the finalization of tenders in an open meeting. So, I made some excuse and was then posted as Special Secretary in the Irrigation Department. I took over on 3rd October 1989.

Elections in the State were due. The Congress lost and a new government under Shri Mulayam Singh Yadav was sworn in. There were wide administrative changes. Shri Shaibal Mukherjee was shifted out and was replaced by

Shri KR Bhatti as Secretary of the Social Welfare Department. The minister of the department was from Faizabad, Shri Awadhesh Prasad. As they always looked for a lady officer for a post like ICDS I soon got my transfer orders as Director ICDS and had to take over on 5th February 1990.

The work of the ICDS Directorate was to provide nutrition to the children who came to the Anganwadi centres which were working in all villages. The Anganwadi worker was a woman of the village and was paid a small honorarium. Her responsibilities included taking care of the children in a pre-nursery type of setting, interact with their mothers to educate them about child welfare and provide them mid day meals. Those days the food served to the children was either chana, bananas, gur, biscuits, etc. Once a fortnight the Auxiliary Nurse Midwife (ANM) who was posted at the primary health centre would come with a weighing machine to weigh the children and tell their mothers about child welfare, health and hygiene, vaccination, nutrition and so on. The system was good in theory but it did not work well in reality due to the rampant corruption.

I had a long discussion with Shri KR Bhatti before I joined. He persuaded me to join as Director ICDS which I did on 5 February 1990. Things were extremely bad not only in the Directorate but also in the field. Everyday would start on a depressing note. There would be a horde of complaints in the morning 'Dak' pertaining to embezzlement of funds, rotten supplies, unpalatable food, absconding Anganwadi workers and ANMs. I myself did several inspections and was shocked to find liquid 'gur' (jaggery) flowing out of the store rooms and rotting bananas. The Anganwadi workers too had begun to mobilize themselves and were asking for a regular salary and the status of a government official. The procurement of the ingredients which went into the making of the nutritious meal for the children was big business. Prior to my joining, when the tenders of the suppliers were opened, there had been firing in the office. It was a very unhealthy and unwholesome atmosphere. You can imagine the mindset of people who could play with funds and supplies meant for children. In this scenario I felt very much ill at ease and wanted to discuss the issues with the Secretary Shri Bhatti.

Shri Bhatti had been a very friendly person before I joined the department, but he completely changed when I started to work with him. He just clamped shut. His attitude was that it is your responsibility and you handle it. Even if I wanted to think aloud and use him as a sounding board he would have none of it. I was very much surprised at the way people change. It was a stroke of good luck when very soon the department was bifurcated into two, Women Welfare Department and Child Welfare Department. While Shri Bhatti remained with only half the original department, Ms Sarla Sahni promoted to the IAS became the Secretary of the Child Welfare Department. She was a very fine person, very supportive, willing to take responsibility and think out of the box. We had perfect team spirit and had the same outlook on various issues.

I particularly remember one telling case during my stint in this department. One of our suppliers had supplied substandard items and the Directorate had withheld his payment. He went to court. During my time as Director I received an order of the High Court bench at Lucknow, which said that the supplier's payment be made by such and such a date and if it is not made then the Director must come personally and appear before the court. Officers did not want to personally appear before the court because they were often humiliated by the judiciary deliberately and I too have experienced it personally on more than one occasion. I, on studying the matter, came to the firm opinion that the payment could not be made and we decided that we would not be brow beaten to make payment for unfit supplies and that I would appear before the court. It was a two member bench, one of the members being Justice Srivastava. When our case came up for hearing and Justice Srivastava put to me the question as to when I was going to make the payment, I informed the court that the payment could not be made. On hearing this Justice Srivastava got annoyed and asked me whether I wanted to go to jail. I was taken aback and our standing counsel asked me not to utter a word and leave the matter to him. You can imagine my shock and outrage when later I saw the order passed by the judges which said that the Director ICDS had agreed to make the payment. I could not believe my eyes. I sent a note to the standing counsel to take up the issue and he too was equally shocked. My respect for the judiciary took a severe beating that day.

I am not aware what finally happened in the case as shortly afterwards I was shifted again. I was however sorry at leaving Ms Sarla Sahni who too shortly retired from service.

Although I left the department I kept in touch with her and continued to meet her frequently till her death. She took on the mafia resulting in complaints and I remember how thoughtlessly a vigilance enquiry was instituted against her. Of course it came to nothing but it did cause her some harassment and humiliation.

7

Special Secretary (Department of Power), Lucknow

AFTER A SHORT stint as Special Secretary (Medical Education), I joined the Department of Power as Special Secretary on August 1990. The Secretary was Shri AK Jain of the 1971 batch and the minister was Shri Lalji Tandon of the BJP.

Shri AK Jain was a very honest officer but he took his honesty to the extreme limit. Although one was allowed tea and biscuits for meetings as and when one held meetings, the Secretary would pay for the tea from his own pocket. When he asked you whether you would like some tea, you normally refused because you would otherwise feel embarrassed when he fished out a fifty paise coin for the tea. He was interested in a posting in Delhi on Central Government deputation. He was not happy in Lucknow and would be gone to Delhi over extended weekends. Consequently I found myself holding the fort for the department. Anyway, he seemed happy to delegate matters to his Special Secretary. Even when the UP State Electricity Board went on strike, Shri Jain was attending a month long training course at Delhi. Very often when the minister called a meeting, Shri Jain would report a bad stomach and send me for the meeting.

One major case on which we disagreed pertained to a retired Chief Engineer (Level II) whose promotion to the grade of Chief Engineer (Level I) had been recommended subject to him being absolved in the vigilance enquiry instituted against him. This matter had now come up for a decision. He had been indicted for financial irregularities and the matter had been referred to the Vigilance Department. The vigilance report had been received in the matter and did not absolve the engineer. If the department did not agree with the report of the Vigilance Department then the department had to refer the case with arguments and justification to a committee headed by the Chief Secretary. I however found no reason to not agree with the report of the Vigilance Department. But even before the matter could come up to the committee, I started getting telephone calls from sundry quarters in favour of the engineer. Officers who had never spoken to me before were calling up to recommend the engineer's case. I refused to take anybody's call. Shri AK Jain was as usual at Delhi and since the Chief Secretary Shri VK Saxena an officer of the 1966 batch had called a meeting at short notice, I had to attend this meeting. The Chief Secretary was not very happy with the department for agreeing with the Vigilance Department. It was obvious that he was interested in promoting the Chief Engineer. He told me to look at the case again and study it further. This was considered hint enough. Another date was given. The Secretary returned but wanted me to attend the meeting which I refused. He then wanted me to change my note. I told him that I had given my views and if he did not agree he could overrule me. There were some very heated arguments. The long and the short of the story is that the engineer could not be promoted and the Chief Secretary too was now unhappy.

The UP State Electricity Board was in dire straits. It was incurring heavy losses and financial institutions were not willing to give it a loan without a government guarantee. The government had decided that it would no longer guarantee the loans. There was rampant corruption and inefficiency. The transmission and distribution losses were more than 40%. The UPSEB was always keen to raise the power tariff which would in effect meant passing the burden of their inefficiency and corruption on to the consumers which was not justified. I felt that they must exercise some austerity measures first. All the engineers of the Power Department whether serving or retired were entitled to free power for life. I put up the matter for ending this practice to the Secretary but it ended up in the Secretary's almirah and died a natural death. There is a lack of courage to support right causes for fear of rocking the boat. You must be a cog in the wheel. Everyone wants that the status quo must continue. That is the policy in the government.

In December '91 I left the Department of Power. All government officers are given the facility of Leave Travel Concession, where the government pays the travel fare for the family to go on holiday anywhere in India. The boarding and lodging however has to be borne by the officer concerned. LTC is given once in a block of four years. It is then normally extended for one more year for officers who were not able to avail of the facility, within the stipulated block, after which grace period it lapses. In December '91 as the grace period of the LTC was lapsing, I had to avail of this facility by December itself. When I broached the subject of leave with the Secretary he informed me that since he would be on leave during that period I could not be allowed leave. Even after explaining to him the circumstances under which it was imperative for me to avail of leave, Shri AK Jain was adamant in denying me leave. I even reminded him that he had already taken leave several times that year and if my LTC was not lapsing I could have postponed it. However when it was apparent that Shri Jain was not in a receptive mood, I sent my application for longer leave which fell in the jurisdiction of the Personnel Department to sanction. My leave was sanctioned by the Personnel Department although Shri Jain tried unsuccessfully to get it cancelled. This is how selfish and petty some officers get. It is one rule for me and a different one for you.

The promotion of my batch to the super time scale was now due and the day I returned from LTC, my personal assistant gave me a copy of the promotion order posting me as Secretary of the Hill Development Department.

8

Secretary (Department of Hill Development)

THE INDIAN Administrative Service in the '90s was in the throes of stagnation due to the induction of large batches. The career trajectory of an IAS officer in the State Secretariat began as a Deputy Secretary and went on to that of Joint Secretary, Special Secretary, Secretary and finally Principal Secretary. The concept of Principal Secretary was relatively new.

The 1976 batch to which I belonged was a big batch of 20 officers. Likewise a few batches senior and a few batches junior were also large batches. There were no vacancies and no avenues for promotion. So the government hit upon the idea of posting the super-time officers who should have been independently handling departments, under a Principal Secretary. So although the officers were promoted as Secretary, their position remained no better than that of a Special Secretary because again the work distribution was done by the Principal Secretary. He might give you important work or some meaningless work, whereas being promoted to the super time scale meant that we had reached a particular threshold in the service and were now competent to handle departments independently as was the case earlier.

I was posted as Secretary (Hill Development) but under a Principal Secretary. Shri Kamakrishna of 1965 batch was the Principal Secretary. Of the 11 sections in the department he allotted me two and I found that some of the special Secretaries who did not even belong to the Indian Administrative Service were handling more important work than I was. He would hold some meeting and I would not be informed. As an afterthought he would send his peon to call me in the midst of the meeting. I found all this very humiliating.

There was no change in status or responsibility even after promotion. One was only designated as a Secretary in name. I made up my mind not to stay long in the department and so after a couple of months I proceeded on leave. I impressed upon the Appointments Department to post me as an independent Secretary of however small a department rather than a Secretary under a Principal Secretary. I wanted to feel free to run the department as I thought fit. It was primarily due to my insistence on this that I was posted as Secretary of departments like Renewable Sources of Energy, Sports, Electronics, Sericulture, Animal Husbandry and Fisheries, Water Resources and so on as against Home, Finance and Industry which had several secretaries under the Principal Secretary. This was till such time as the government began to club three or four Principal Secretaries under one Commissioner, like the Agriculture and Rural Development Department under the Agricultural Production Commissioner, Small Industries, Heavy Industries, Exports etc. under the Industrial Development Commissioner and so on. Consequently the status of even the Principal Secretaries was downgraded.

9

Executive Director (SIFPSA), UP

MRS SUMITA Kandpal who had earlier been my boss in Jhansi was looking for an officer who could handle the new USAID project for family planning in UP. She was at this time Principal Secretary Health and Family Welfare. She asked me whether I would be willing to join her as the Director of this agency which was named as State Innovations in Family Planning Services Agency (SIFPSA). SIFPSA's role was to facilitate through innovative means and partnerships with government and other agencies, the goal of health for all by improving the quality, demand, access and delivery of family planning and mother and child health services. I knew that this project would involve very hard work and discomfort as it had yet to take off. I would have to begin by even registering the society. But I took it as a challenge and on the 12th February 1993 I joined as Director SIFPSA.

SIFPSA was yet to take off the ground. Besides me as the Director, Principal Secretary (Health and Family Welfare) as the Vice Chairman and the Chief Secretary designated as the Chairman, there was no other staff, no office, no infrastructural support and no money even to pay my salary. After some time, I was given additional charge of the post of Director of the State Institute of Health and Family Welfare in order to facilitate matters. This was done to provide me with a place to sit and basic infrastructural support to help establish SIFPSA. I registered the society namely SIFPSA which was registered under the Societies Registration Act 1963. The work of framing rules and manuals of the society was carried out with the help of Tata Consultancy Services, an office building was hired, schemes were formulated, some staff was recruited, vehicles were bought and familiarization sessions for the DMs and the Chief Medical Officers for all the districts of UP were organized at the Indian Institute of Management, Lucknow in batches where I personally briefed them in detail about the project. All this work was done single-handedly in less than a year's time. I really had to rough it out for the first six months without any salary because it was only after six months of red tapism that even the State Institute could pay me my arrears. These were to be later reimbursed to the State Institute of Health and Family Welfare by SIFPSA when funds were received in the project.

I took up this job as a challenge. Every paper and note in this office had to be personally dictated by me. After a year of hard work, things began to fall into place. The basic infrastructure and framework were in place for the project to start taking off. But on a Saturday which was a holiday and offices were closed, I was dictating the agenda notes for the next Board meeting when I received a letter transferring me from the post of Director SIFPSA to that of Joint Managing Director of the Mahila Kalyan Nigam (Women's Welfare Corporation). I was stunned. Here I was breaking my back setting up the project and just as things had begun to settle and move forward, I was given marching orders. This came to me as a bolt from the blue because I was working directly with the Chief Secretary and if he wanted to shift me, for whatever reason, he could have at least given me an inkling. I was meeting him officially every other day.

It took me some time to get over my shock and extreme anger. I sought an appointment with the Chief Secretary Shri TSR Subramanian of the 1961 batch. He told me that he had no complaints against me and that I had done very good work and so on. I told him in no uncertain terms that he had made a fool of me. When there was nothing in the project and no takers for the job, I slogged it out and as soon as there was some basic infrastructure, teething problems had been overcome and things had started moving forward, I was unceremoniously thrown out like this. I also informed him that I would not be able to join the Mahila Kalyan Nigam. I requested him for a change. He told me to first join and that he would see what could be done thereafter.

Soon enough there was a call from Mrs Uma Pillai of the 1968 batch who had been posted in my place. She told me that she had been told to join immediately. I requested her to give me a couple of days to get my new posting diverted. I had planned to meet the Chief Minister and ask him for a change of posting. Mrs Uma Pillai, however, felt she could not afford to take a risk and on 24th May itself came to the office in my absence and took over in absentia. It was clear from her attitude and behaviour that she was keen on the SIFPSA job and had got me ousted. She was known to be close to the Chief Secretary. Her husband Shri HD Pillai from the IPS was also a friend of Shri TSR Subramanian.

Prior to this there had been another incident where Shri TSR Subramanian and the Pillais had rubbed us on the wrong side. A Type-V house was allotted to us in Dilkhusha Colony by Shri KK Jaiswal (1968 batch) who was the then PWD Secretary in UP and the occupant of that house. Shri Jaiswal was going on deputation to Government of India. We had to wait several months for the house to fall vacant but the day the house fell vacant and Shri Jaiswal's baggage was being loaded, Shri TSR Subramanian changed the allotment order which was in my name to that of Mrs Pillai. We felt thoroughly cheated. So much for the justice and fair play of Shri TSR Subramanian!

The whole episode of SIFPSA left a very bitter taste in my mouth. I felt that I had been taken undue advantage of. Shri TSR Subramanian made me do all the donkey's work and sidelined me without a thought when it suited him. Mrs Kandpal had later informed me that Shri TSR Subramanian was unhappy on my submitting to him a file for the sanction orders for an AC to be installed in his camp office. I do not remember this as it was a petty routine matter. All files pertaining to financial sanction were to be put up to the Chairman, as no sanctioning powers had been delegated to me by the Board. Financial powers vested only with the Chairman and the Board. Still it was surprising that such a matter could be the reason for my ouster.

I met the Chief Minister Shri Mulayam Singh Yadav and told him my problem. He asked me the reason for the Chief Secretary's anger. I told him that I didn't know but that the Chief Minister could make his own enquiries about me and my work. Shri Mulayam Singh promised to look into the matter but when nothing happened even after a week, I once again asked for an appointment to meet him. He remembered my case at once and said that he had made enquiries about me and found that I enjoyed a good reputation. He promised to shortly do something. He also told me that the Chief Secretary Shri TSR Subramanian was insistent that I should first comply with my original transfer order and then ask for a change. I on the other hand was saying that when I could not work in that organization (and I had very valid reasons for the same), it seemed foolish to join in the first place. Sure enough, transfer orders posting me as the Secretary of the Department of Non-Conventional Energy now known as the Department of Renewable Sources of Energy issued shortly thereafter. Shri TSR Subramanian too was soon thereafter, removed from the post of Chief Secretary. Shri TSR Subramanian is often seen on TV channels holding forth about the bureaucracy. I want to ask him whether his dealings with me were in conformity with the principles of justice and fair play, he so vociferously now expresses on TV!

Another incident that I would like to recall pertaining to my SIFPSA posting was that Mrs Uma Pillai did not even allow me to take my just dues. The manuals prepared by the Tata Consultancy Services regarding the personal, procurement, financial and other systems entitled the officers to certain perks like reimbursement to some extent of electricity bills, education allowance for children, servants allowance and other sundry facilities. These manuals had been approved by the Board but I had not drawn them as yet, as I was too busy with my official schedule to look at personal issues. As all my dues were being reimbursed by SIFPSA to the State Institute of Health and Family Welfare and as my substantive posting was in SIFPSA, I should have got these facilities from the date of my joining SIFPSA. As I was relieved in absentia by Mrs Uma Pillai, I had no time to settle these matters while still in the job. I wrote to the Chairman that I should be given my arrears. However I got a letter from Mrs Uma Pillai that I was not entitled to any benefits with retrospective effect. I represented against this decision which I felt was unjust. I could not succeed.

When Shri Mata Prasad of the 1960 batch became the Chief Secretary, I took up the matter with him. His attitude was bizarre. He asked me as to why I should be given the arrears as I according to his information belonged to a wealthy family from Meerut. I told him that if that was his argument then the government should not give me a salary either. Shri Mata Prasad was succeeded as the Chief Secretary by Shri Brijendra Sahai of the 1961 batch. When things just would not go forward I sent him a letter giving notice that if my dues were not given to me I would have no recourse but to approach the court and finally I did. My case came up and the order was given in my favour but when SIFPSA still did not pay my dues, I decided to file for contempt of court. In the meanwhile, believe it or not, the judgement changed on the basis of review filed by the government without any notice to me. This was shocking and I came to know that the then Chief Secretary Shri Yogendra Narain of the 1965 batch discussed the issue with the Legal Remembrancer, who in turn reportedly approached the judge who reversed his judgement. The judge concerned was Justice PC Verma who later came in for a lot of flak.

10

Secretary (Department of Non-Conventional Energy)

I TOOK over as Secretary, Non-Conventional Energy in 1994. Although I had some very short tenures, I stayed in this department for more than two years and enjoyed the work pertaining to the dissemination of solar, wind and biomass energy. The best thing about this job was that it was an independent department. There was no Principal Secretary above me. I only had a minister and in this case the minister happened to be the Chief Minister himself. The department had an agency to implement the schemes. It was called NEDA (Non-Conventional Energy Development Agency) of which the Secretary of the department was also the ex-officio Chairman.

Popularization of Renewable sources of energy was at that time in a nascent stage but in the early '90s UP had already taken a lead. Two grid interactive solar power plants of 100 kW capacity had been set-up on an experimental basis, one each at Aligarh and Azamgarh. These gave us insights into future developments. The programs like distribution of solar lanterns, electrification of villages by solar lights, distribution of solar cookers, pressure cookers were being run. The IREP (Integrated Rural Energy Programme) was also being funded by the Government of India. I issued policies for buy-back of power from renewable sources of energy by the government at pre-determined rates. This provided a great boost to the development of renewable source of energy, particularly of biomass. All sugar factories began to produce electricity through their biomass and this was one programme which began to do extremely well. It would, of course, have done much better if the UP State Electricity Board had cooperated more.

I will narrate a few instances which show the vested interests and pettiness everywhere in the government. In the mid-'90s NEDA was also distributing pressure cookers at a high subsidy. Pressure cookers had become very common by then even in the villages. I felt there was no need to subsidize pressure cookers but I found a lot of resistance from the staff dealing with this programme. Although I did stop the programme during my time I found that after I had left, they had got the programme restarted. It was obvious that the staff had vested interests. It was also a very difficult task to verify on the ground whether pressure cookers were actually being distributed.

In 1996 Shri RS Mathur of the 1965 batch of the IAS who was Principal Secretary, Power Department at the time was suddenly made Principal Secretary Non-Conventional Sources of Energy also. So far I was handling the department independently. Just a couple of months back I had bought a new vehicle for the department. As the traditional Ambassador car which had a very long delivery period, I bought a Fiat NE that had just come into the market. This was the first different car ever bought in the Secretariat. All cars hitherto were Ambassadors. Shri RS Mathur on taking over as Principal Secretary wanted this vehicle. Instead of looking to the bigger issues, Shri Mathur began eyeing the vehicle I was using. There was no dearth of cars at Shri Mathur's disposal but he still wanted the Fiat and took it although I had been using it for several months. He was the Principal Secretary of a huge department but he did not think twice about humiliating me.

In February '96 I had been nominated by the Department of Renewable Sources, Government of India, to participate in a study tour of some projects in Australia and New Zealand. After Shri RS Mathur took over he tried his best to get my name removed and go himself. Although he did not succeed in replacing me, I certainly did not appreciate his efforts in that direction.

The trip to Australia and New Zealand was another story altogether. The programme in Australia and New Zealand on behalf of TERI (Tata Energy Research Institute) was being coordinated in Hobart, the capital of Tasmania by one local resident Shri Sharma and another IAS officer Shri Mathur who had accompanied us from TERI. A couple of times Shri Sharma informally hosted lunch at his residence. We were appreciating his hospitality before we realized that he was using our daily allowance to entertain us. We were surprised when we were not given our full Dearness Allowance (DA).

On making enquiries we were told that as a couple of meals had been provided by Shri Sharma, that money was to be reimbursed to the latter. We all felt that this was unethical and so we complained to the Department of Renewable Sources of Energy. I also wrote to the Director of TERI Shri RK Pachauri. It was with great difficulty and constant persistence that I was able to get the full DA, thanks to the efforts of Dr SK Chopra who was Senior Advisor and Additional Secretary in the Ministry of Renewable Sources of Energy. If we are wronged, we should take up the issue, however small. It is our acceptance of wrongs that gives others the courage to keep on doing them.

I would like to mention here that while I was taking up the issue I had also written to the Ministry of Finance, on which the Chief Secretary of UP Shri Mata Prasad pulled me up for writing to the Government of India directly. TERI perhaps had complained. He seemed to have forgotten that I was heading the department and corresponded with the Central Government on a regular basis. In government, speaking up, raising your voice against any injustice, firmness and determination to see such issues to a conclusion are not appreciated. You must be flexible and tolerant. 'Chalta hai' is the right attitude. A no-nonsense officer particularly a lady officer is not appreciated.

11

Secretary (Sports)

FROM THE Department of Non-Conventional Energy I was posted as Secretary of the Department of Sports in July '96. I took over with some difficulty from Shri Shashank Shekhar Singh, a pilot who rose to become Principal Secretary (Civil Aviation). From there as his base he had begun to make further inroads into the service by managing to add to his portfolio, some smaller departments like tourism or sports which would not raise too many eyebrows. He made many officers feel obliged to him by providing them free rides in the State aircrafts.

Now the Sports Department was divested from Shri S Shekhar Singh and given to me. This was a small and neglected department and nobody wanted to be posted there. When I joined, there was only one Section Officer under me. I worked for a month as independent Secretary of the department but in a little over a months' time Shri S Shekhar Singh who was obviously smarting from having the Sports Department taken away from his charge, managed to get himself posted once again as Principal Secretary Sports. As no orders for my transfer issued, it was obvious that I was to work under him. This was not acceptable to me. I found this extremely humiliating. After 20 years of service and having held independent charge of departments more important than sports, I was not going to work under a Principal Secretary and that too under a person like Shri Shashank Shekhar Singh who had no credentials except his political connections and manipulations.

I wrote to the Chief Secretary and to the UP IAS Officers Association questioning the propriety of a super-time scale officer with more than 20 years of service working under Shri Shashank Shekhar Singh. I also highlighted how many senior Principal Secretary level officers from the IAS were holding charge of only one department while Shri Shashank Shekhar Singh was holding charge of three departments. Even if we accepted his expertise in the Civil Aviation sector, what was his expertise in other sectors like that of Non-Conventional Energy, Sports etc.

I requested that his orders for Sports be cancelled. Finally his orders were cancelled with great difficulty and I continued to work as independent Secretary. Shri Shashank Shekhar Singh could not forgive me for this and when he became the Cabinet Secretary in May 2007 during Ms Mayawati's Chief Ministership, his vengeance culminated in my suspension from service in September 2012.

12

Food Commissioner (Uttar Pradesh)

I BECAME Food Commissioner of UP on 7th November 1996. This was the main subordinate office of the Department of Food and Civil Supplies. The main duty of the Food Commissioner was to ensure the procurement of food grains and their supply to and proper management of the ration shops in the State. When I joined as Food Commissioner, Principal Secretary of the department was Shri SN Shukla of the 1968 batch of the IAS. He had a clean image and was known as an honest and upright officer, though a difficult boss. Knowing him to be honest, I did not foresee any difficulty in working with him.

The year 1996 once again saw drought in UP and the prices of wheat sky-rocketed. Amidst complaints of shortage of food grains and constant travails of the poor, the department was hard pressed to tackle the situation urgently. Adding to this the constant refrain of the media about the shortage of wheat flour to the poor made things worse. Normally only grains are distributed from ration shops but that year to combat the situation we embarked on a scheme of marketing flour at controlled rates. This scheme was to be restricted to the poorest of the poor, so that the scheme was not misused. The Department of Food and Civil Supplies decided that the beneficiaries of this scheme should be given new ration cards. As the matter was urgent we immediately embarked upon the task of getting these new ration cards printed at the Government Press at Allahabad. The Regional Food Controller of the Allahabad Division was given the prime responsibility of ensuring that these ration cards were printed and distributed within a couple of days. The following events relating to the issue of these ration cards shows clearly how the government often wastes its time and energy on useless matters.

Shri SN Shukla, Principal Secretary of the Department of Food, personally wanted to see a sample of the ration card which was being printed. The ration card was faxed from Allahabad to my office and I in turn faxed it to the Secretary's office. As this was a time of emergency and time was of the essence, the preparations for issuing the cards were continued simultaneously. The Secretary however desired that the ration card should have on it the picture of a poor man. It would again take time but still the Secretary's comments were relayed back to the Regional Food Controller for incorporating the addition. When the rectified sample came from Allahabad, I forwarded it to the Secretary with the remark that his orders had been complied with. You can imagine mine and the other officers bewilderment when the card came back with the remark that "a below poverty line man does not look so healthy." We seemed to be getting bogged down in inane details, totally irrelevant to the implementation of the scheme. A ration card anyway in a month's time would become dirty, tattered and hardly recognizable. However, keeping in mind the Secretary's written orders I had no alternative but to pass on the comments for the rectification of the image once again. A picture of an emaciated man with hollow cheeks was imprinted on the ration card and sent to the Secretary directly. The card came back with the comments that "his ears are too big." Things just seemed to have slipped out of hand. It seemed that we were in the process of 'designing' a ration card! I was worried because I as the Commissioner would be held responsible for any delay pertaining to the execution of the scheme. Finally we just ignored these comments and concentrated on the more important issues relating to the distribution of the cards and supply of flour. It is very difficult to function in a set-up where we can get into such useless and inane trivialities. An extremely important issue was degenerating into a laughing matter!

There were other continuous irritants from the Secretary. I soon started getting letters questioning my style of functioning. He would want to know why I had called a meeting of my Regional Food Controllers and District Supply Officers at Lucknow and not at the various divisional headquarters. I informed him that since time was of the essence and I had just taken over, I wanted to meet all my officers at the earliest. In a week's time I had met everybody whereas if I was to go on tour to all the divisions it would take me a couple of months. As we were in the midst of a crisis I needed to interact with my officers immediately. I told him also that he would be well within his rights to question me on my targets and achievements but that he could not question me as to where I held a meeting or complain that my officers were very often sitting in my room and so on and so forth.

I immediately realized within a month of my joining that it would be impossible for me to function in this department given the attitude of Shri SN Shukla and that it would be best to quit before three months were over. A lot of time is spent in the government on irrelevant matters which have no bearing on the work. There is undue interference in the subordinate offices from the Secretariat. The departments in the Secretariat have all the information pertaining to the schemes but in spite of this, any time a letter is received for a meeting or any information is desired by another department, they simply send it to the subordinate offices without turning the pages in their own files. Even draft letters are required to be sent by the subordinate offices. This has resulted in a situation where instead of doing constructive work, the subordinate offices are most of the time acting like maids in waiting to the department. Instead of looking at the implementation and execution of the schemes by their field officers, they find themselves spoon feeding the department. Work and efficiency has suffered severely as a result. At the drop of a hat the officers in the subordinate offices are summoned to the Secretariat to help them out with their work and spend hours there everyday.

13

Secretary (Department of Electronics)

IN 1997 I was appointed as Secretary of the Department of Electronics, and I worked as Secretary of that department for a year. It was an independent department and I was reporting directly to the Chief Secretary. The Chief Secretary was Shri RS Mathur of 1965 batch of whom I spoken earlier and the minister of the department was Raja Aridaman Singh.

Major corporation under the Department of Electronics was Uptron, manufacturer of the Uptron TV sets. Private entrepreneurship however had taken hold of the electronics sector and the government sector Uptron was finding the going tough. Neither were they able to take quick commercial decisions nor keep pace with the developments the sector was showing. Uptron was also a victim of the same malady and although it had made its mark in the initial days, it was now accruing heavy losses. The corporation was not in a position to pay the salaries of the employees and the salaries had not been paid for the last six months. Approximately

30-40% of the staff had resigned and left for better pastures while some others had managed to go on deputation to other departments. It could be said that the staff that remained back with the corporation included the less efficient ones who were unable to get another job. Some of the remaining staff had also taken up part time jobs to get some income. The company was in such a situation that it incurred loss on anything that it produced. The matter for its rehabilitation was pending before the BIFR for quite some time. We even thought of introducing a scheme for voluntary retirement of the staff but it could not go forward because the company did not have any funds for the same. I was convinced that Uptron was a dead horse and must be closed.

It was a really bad time for the company. The Chairman of Uptron Shri AK Rastogi of the 1966 batch, had been a very high profile officer. He had worked as the Home Secretary, under Shri Mulayam Singh Yadav before the Babri Masjid demolition. Unfortunately he had had a stroke after that and was not in the best physical condition and so was adjusted as Chairman, Uptron. Uptron was an irretrievably sick company and the workers had not received their salaries for several months. They were unhappy when they found that Shri Rastogi was reimbursing the expenditure on bananas, oranges and grapes from the office. Around the same time the Managing Director Shri Ashok Kumar of the 1982 batch also unfortunately committed suicide.

As Uptron was situated in Lucknow and the Member of Parliament from there was Shri Atal Bihari Vajpayee of the BJP, the workers would now and then approach him and he had begun to actively espouse the case of Uptron. Two weeks after I joined the department, Shri Atal Bihari Vajpayee got a meeting organized in Delhi under the Chairmanship of the then Prime Minister Shri HD Deve Gowda. He was demanding a rehabilitation package for Uptron from the Government of India. I and the Finance Secretary of UP Shri VK Mittal attended the meeting at the Prime Minister's residence in Delhi. As was expected the Central Government was not agreeable to giving any funds for Uptron's rehabilitation.

The only thing that occupied the department at that time was the matter of Uptron. The amount required for its rehabilitation was too heavy. The BIFR had also been dragging its feet over the issue for a very long time. I discussed this issue with the minister who was convinced with my arguments to put up the matter for its closure in the cabinet. We spent a couple of weeks on making the cabinet note. The comments of the Law Department and the Finance Department were included in the cabinet note as is required. The Chief Minister at the time was Shri Kalyan Singh. The file was sent to him through the Chief Secretary but it came back with some query which was answered and the matter was again put up for inclusion in the agenda for the cabinet.

This was considered a gross mistake. It was unthinkable that Shri Kalyan Singh would take up the issue of closure of Uptron when Shri Atal Bihari Vajpayee was supporting the employees union. I was looking solely at the merits of the case and gave no thought to the political repercussions of such a decision. The file thereafter did not return but I immediately got transfer orders and was posted as the Secretary of the General Administration Department. This department was only a parking slot for officers out of favour. It did not even have a vehicle for the Secretary and its only work happened to be declaration of national holidays and mourning when a VVIP passed away. I tried to meet the Chief Minister Shri Kalyan Singh over a period of several months but did not get an appointment.

I still feel that the decision I took to close Uptron was the right decision. The earlier hard decisions are taken the better it is. Uptron, I heard, dragged on for several years in a pitiable state incurring still heavier losses before it was finally closed.

14

Secretary (Land Resources and Water Management)

I NEXT joined as Secretary of the Department of Land Resources and Water Management. I worked in this department for exactly 3 weeks. I joined on 1st April 1999 and I handed over on 21st April 1999. The minister of the department was Shri Mandaleshwar Singh. When I joined the department the minister was on tour. I left message in his office that I had taken over and wanted to call on him. I left instructions with his Personal Secretary that he should let me know immediately as and when the minister returned and attended office.

I had some experience in this sector of water management as I had a stint as Joint Administrator of the Ramganga Command Area Development project. There were three command areas under the control of this department namely—the Sharda Sahayak project, Ramganga Command Area project and the Gandak project. These projects were basically for improving the water management in the command areas of these rivers. Except for the Gandak project the Administrators of both the Sharda Sahayak project and the Ramganga Command Area project were senior officers belonging to 1973 and 1974 batches respectively.

It was more than two weeks when the minister finally gave me time. I also came to know that the minister had in fact come to the office a week earlier before again leaving on tour but had not bothered to give me an appointment at that time. I had a fairly long meeting with him in which I shared my vision for the department and my experiences in the Ramganga Command Area project. This meeting seemed cordial enough. He made all the right noises and also complained against some of the officers. However within a couple of days of this meeting I got my transfer orders from the department.

This was my shortest stint ever till that time in any job. I was wondering why I had been transferred out. There was as yet nothing on which there had been any disagreement with the minister nor had I given him any occasion to be annoyed. There seemed no cause for his unhappiness. I was therefore very curious to know the reason for the sudden shift in such a short time. I came to know from the Chief Minister's office that my minister had been sitting on dharna in the Chief Minister's office, begging Shri Kalyan Singh that I should be shifted out as I didn't 'suit' him. He was also heard saying that if the Chief Minister heeded this request of his, he would never ask him for another favour. Shri Kalyan Singh acquiesced and I was shifted out of the department. Just about an hour's interaction with the minister, perhaps made him realize that I might not do his biddings and so he declared that I would not 'suit' him.

15

Secretary (Sericulture)

AFTER THE extremely short stint in Land Resources and Water Management I was kept in waiting for a week without a posting. Finally I took over as Secretary and Director Sericulture from 1st May 1999 and worked there also only for six months. My department was under the Agricultural Production Commissioner who was also ex-officio Additional Chief Secretary. He headed the entire rural development set-up of the government. The post at that time was being held by Shri Sant Kumar Tripathi of the 1967 batch. He was my immediate reporting officer and important policy files were submitted to the minister through him. Shri Sardar Singh, Minister for Sericulture, was an MLA from Mathura. He was also the Minister for Handlooms.

Sericulture is not very popular in UP. The climate in UP is not very conducive for sericulture, unlike in Karnataka where the farmers harvest several crops and it happens to be a very viable and profitable option for them. In UP, the Sericulture Department had its own sericulture farms which were a drain on the State exchequer and had no relevance to the propagation of sericulture in the State. The department was spending a lot of money on the upkeep and maintenance of these farms but was getting no return whatsoever. The labourers who were working on these farms were raising the cocoons, harvesting them and marketing them for themselves. I was convinced at that time that this was one department which the government should think of closing down. Its activities and the results thereof did not merit a separate department. As a beginning however, I did extensive research and prepared a proposal for selling the sericulture farms but such proposals never see the light of day.

When I joined the Department of Sericulture, municipal elections in the State were due and the model code of conduct had come into force. This in fact meant that after the notification of polls and till the process of election is complete, restrictions would be in force for the ministers who could not use their official position for party work. But in spite of this and soon thereafter our minister Shri Sardar Singh sent a request that his return ticket to Delhi be booked and paid for by the Sericulture Directorate. This is not the practice even at normal times, as tickets for ministers are booked by the Secretariat Administration Department and not by individual departments. We heard that Shri Sardar Singh was in the habit of getting tickets booked and paid for by the subordinate offices while at the same time reimbursing those TA bills from the Secretariat Administration Department. I was told that at that time he had already raised bills of more than ₹ 1.5 lakh in the Handloom Corporation. As the minister was insistent that his tickets be booked by the Directorate, we took up the matter with the Secretariat Administration Department which informed us that they were still continuing to give advance to ministers for their tickets. Under the circumstances it was surprising that the minister was pressurizing us to buy the tickets. As the minister's intention I presumed was to make money, he made all sorts of excuses, even going to the extent of saying that he had forgotten the coupons given by the Secretariat Administration at home. Finally we informed him that his staff could book the ticket through a travel agency and the payment could be made by him later. He was very annoyed. Battle lines had been drawn.

As I was both the Secretary of the department and also the Director my normal routine was to sit in the Secretariat in the mornings and in the Directorate in the afternoons. The very next day, after the above incident, the minister reached the Directorate at 10 o'clock in the morning for inspection. Ministers did not land up in the subordinate offices without information and unescorted by any officer. There is a certain protocol that is normally followed. He should have informed me about his programme but he did not. I was told that he made a big Tamasha (Show) by putting a lock on the gate and sitting outside, to ensure that no late-comers could enter. The office incidentally was in a residential area and this generated a lot of interest among the neighbours. I was informed that the minister shouted at the staff and misbehaved thoroughly. He called the Director's Personal Secretary and asked him how much money he had helped an ex-Director to make and so on. I would like to mention here that the Directorate was also implementing a World Bank project of ₹ 62 crore albeit with little success. The minister would keep mentioning this amount. The same day he also made the remark to the Personal Secretary as narrated to me afterwards, "62 crores par sabki nazar lagi hui hai. Dekh loonga." (Everybody has his eyes on 62 crores. I will see). Obviously it was he who had his eyes on that money!

Around the same time action was initiated against a few members of the staff who were involved in irregular activities and also happened to be close to the minister. This also made the minister very angry. He would ring up the Directorate every other day and abuse the junior officers. He made it a habit of suddenly arriving at the Directorate without any intimation. Often I would get calls from the Directorate that they had been informed that the minister would come. I refused to take cognizance of such messages, as the protocol is that the minister or his staff should inform the head of the office about the minister's programme either on telephone or in writing. However this was never done. So I just ignored his visits.

One of the Deputy Directors who was close to the minister was involved in serious financial irregularities. He was transferred out of Lucknow so that the enquiry could proceed without hindrance. Shri Sardar Singh however had a very soft spot for this officer as the latter had ingratiated himself to him by supplying, as I came to know, groceries and provisions for his household. This came to knowledge as one day the office intercepted a hand written note sent by the personal secretary of the minister mentioning oil, masalas, gas cylinders to be supplied to the minister's residence. It was obvious that these provisions were being sent to the minister's residence by some officer in the Directorate. The letter was torn and thrown away. The minister told me to stay the transfer of this Deputy Director. I explained to the minister that it would be very difficult to conduct an enquiry against the officer if he was present in the office. He could even have been suspended but he had only been transferred so that the enquiry could proceed without hindrance.

The minister however kept pressurizing me to cancel the transfer order. Totally frustrated, the minister one day at about 1.30 PM reached my office at the Directorate without any prior information. I was present in the Directorate at that time. He was shouting at the top of his voice and I could hear some commotion outside. My peon came running in to inform me that the minister had come. The door opened and I came to the door to receive the minister, made him comfortable on the sofa and asked him why he had troubled himself when he could have summoned me. He looked vaguely here and there before he came up with the real reason for his visit. He again brought up the subject of cancellation of the transfer order of the Deputy Director. I pleaded with him about my difficulty and told him that I will get the enquiry completed in record time. Again the minister was not amenable to reason. It was obvious that he had come for a showdown. He was shouting in a loud voice. It was a very embarrassing situation. I had to ask him to speak a little softer as everybody outside could hear and it did not behove the dignity and decorum of a government office. I told him that if he wanted, the facts of the case could be given to him in writing. He said that I had precipitated jungle raj in the office and everybody was afraid of me. When he didn't stop ranting I finally told him that if he did not approve of my style of functioning then he could talk to the Chief Minister for my transfer, but that it was below my dignity to argue with him in this fashion. At this he said yes yes he will speak to the Chief Minister but made some insulting comments. He said "Jaiye jaiye apki do kaudi ki izzat hai. Aap apne aap ko samajhti kya hain" (Go go you have no respect worth the name. Who do you think you are?) As soon as he uttered these words I called for my car and left my office, leaving the minister sitting alone. I was told later by my staff that the minister was shell-shocked at being thus humiliated. He looked as if he was going to have a heart attack. He was given water and made to rest. Obviously he had mistakenly felt that he could bully me into agreeing.

I brought this matter immediately to the notice of the Chief Secretary Shri Yogendra Narain and the UP IAS Officers Association. The Chief Secretary was sympathetic and said that I had been unlucky in getting a minister like that. He asked me to write a strong note detailing the minister's statement and behaviour. I put all the facts of the interaction on record adding that it was impossible for me to function in the department for a minute more. Soon I received my transfer orders as Director, State Planning Institute.

The problems I was facing with the minister were well-known also to my immediate officer the Agricultural Production Commissioner through whom the files were sent to the minister. Reviewing the progress of the scheme known as the Poorvanchal Resham Vikas Pariyojana, I found that a substantial amount of money had been embezzled. There was no mulberry plantation in the field. At the same time this scheme had come up for a further extension of one year. But on review I felt that the accounts should be settled, the scheme closed and a high level enquiry should be instituted. The minister Shri Sardar Singh sent the file back with the remarks that responsibility should be fixed but the scheme must be continued. I wrote back that the responsibility had already been fixed and action against one Additional Director on deputation from the Central Silk Board had been proposed. Moreover this Additional Director who was already on extended deputation should be repatriated to his parent department with immediate effect. The matter was put up to the minister for his approval but he refused. I would like to mention here that this Additional Director's elder brother Shri Ashok Bajpai was an MLA (Member of Legislative Assembly) at that time and shortly afterwards was to become a minister. He also met me and requested that his brother should not be sent back. He was informed that we had nothing personal against his brother but that performance was of the utmost importance. I sent the file again to the minister through the Agricultural Production Commissioner to reconsider his orders. The Agricultural Production Commissioner as I have mentioned earlier was Shri Sant Tripathi of the 1967 batch. It was very interesting to read the Agricultural Production Commissioner's note on the file which said that the minister's views are clearly stated on page number such and such and that "Mantriji ki mansha spasht hai atah kyo ki sachiv vishesh bal de rahi hai atah mamla punah mantriji ko bheja ja raha hai" (minister's intentions are clear but because the Secretary is laying special emphasis on the matter, therefore the matter is being put up to the minister again). The Agricultural Production Commissioner is ex-officio Additional Chief Secretary. From a man of his seniority this kind of note was not expected. We are not here to work according to the Mantri's wish. We are here to give the right advice. The Agricultural Production Commissioner gave the minister the cue. He simply wrote that his previous orders were clear. I would like to mention here that the matter of repatriating the Additional Director had been discussed with the minister earlier and he had agreed to send him back but in the meantime these several episodes had taken place which annoyed the minister. He began to take the opposite view of anything I proposed. He wrote that it was in the interest of work to retain the concerned officer. The minister further started interfering in the work by issuing orders that the concerned officer should be given two peons, one personal assistant and four technical assistants and so on. He began to interfere in matters with which he was not in the least concerned. It was obvious that these letters were being written at the behest of the officer.

The minister felt frustrated that his Secretary was not on the same wavelength as him. He was expressing frustration by shouting around and making abominable statements. The calibre and the values of these politicians is extremely low and shows in their day-to-day transactions and behaviour. Not only do they not do any constructive work, they hamper you also from doing anything. You just get caught up in their vested interests. In UP it is rare to find politicians who think beyond themselves. They want to become politicians and ministers only for the perks, the power and the money. My colleague the Secretary (Handlooms) who also had Shri

Sardar Singh as his minister too was extremely unhappy with him. He told me that Shri Sardar Singh went to Banaras and asked the regional officer there as to how much money he had collected for the Secretary (Handlooms). This is the level of these ministers and they think that everybody is like them. He was informed that the Secretary had, in fact even paid for the dinner that he ate at the guest house. This is the level of many ministers with whom one has to work in UP. How can you expect results?

16

Secretary (Department of Higher Education)

I JOINED as Secretary of the Department of Higher Education on 3rd November 1999. The Principal Secretary was Shri VK Mittal of 1968 batch. Shri Mittal was a very nervous person. He was averse to taking any responsibility and signing files. At the same time he was also unable to resist any pressure. It was well-known that he was a difficult boss.

To prove the case in point I recall that a Joint Secretary in the Chief Minister's office would talk to him now and then about the promotion of a teacher to the next senior grade. Whenever the Joint Secretary called the Principal Secretary Shri Mittal, the latter would immediately call me up in a state of great excitability to ask about the progress in the matter. It is well-known that the department suddenly cannot promote one teacher in isolation. It would entail a departmental promotion committee meeting, preparation for which takes time. One day when Shri Mittal rang up to ask me about this matter saying that the Joint Secretary in the Chief Minister's office (whose name I don't recall) had just spoken to him and wanted to know the progress, I told Shri Mittal that I will personally speak to the Joint Secretary to the Chief Minister and brief him. I rang up the Joint Secretary and took him to task for pressurizing us like this when he himself would know that preparation for the Departmental Promotion Committee (DPC) takes time. After this there were no further calls from the Chief Minister's office pertaining to this particular case. Shri Mittal could have shown some maturity and behaved in keeping with his seniority. Very often junior officers in the Chief Minister's office take undue advantage of the fact that any call from the Chief Minister's Secretariat will elicit immediate panic and response. The Joint Secretary to the Chief Minister could most probably also be pursuing his own personal interests.

During the three four months that I worked with Shri Mittal the latter changed my work distribution four times. Initially, I was also looking after the administration of the department. I found it necessary to transfer one of the Section Officer to another section in the interest of work. There was pressure from sundry sources to post him back to the same section, obviously because the Section Officer had a vested interest in that particular work. I refused but unfortunately Shri Mittal could not withstand the pressure and as he knew that I would not compromise he removed administration from my charge. In a similar fashion whenever I took some action which he did not like he would change my work distribution. He began to bypass me and deal directly with my Special Secretary. I think he felt more comfortable dealing with my junior officer particularly in cases in which he felt that I may not agree. This constant change in work distribution every couple of weeks was very irksome. I felt I was wasting my time here and I met the Chief Secretary Shri Yogendra Narain (1965 batch) about the matter and asked for a change. I also wrote to the Chief Secretary bringing all these facts to his notice. I felt that Shri Mittal would write adversely in my confidential report so I thought it best to put on record, the facts of the case from my point of view.

Shortly afterwards when I joined the Department of Animal Husbandry and Fisheries in early 2000 I found another facet of Shri Mittal's personality. I was informed that our Directorate of Fisheries was functioning from a house in Gomti Nagar which belonged to Shri VK Mittal. Looking at the relationship I had with Shri Mittal nobody would have found fault if I had cancelled our lease and vacated his premises. However, I felt that I at least should not behave in a petty manner. Our relationship was strained and we were not on talking terms. But at a dinner one night where both of us happened to be invited, I was surprised to find Shri VK Mittal coming up to where I was sitting, greet me and talk to me in very cordial terms. It was only later I realized why he had behaved so differently. Of course, he was afraid that the fisheries department may vacate his premises. Leasing your house to the government was a very paying proposition!

Surprisingly, Shri VK Mittal, in spite of our differences did not give me any adverse remarks but just graded me as 'good' which is as good as bad but an officer gives it to avoid a representation by the junior officer which leads to allegations and counter allegations. Years later I was communicated Shri Yogendra Narain's remarks as the reviewing authority of Shri Mittal's remarks. He had remarked that I could do with a little more of team spirit which I found rather surprising. Shri Yogendra Narain was fully in the know of the situation at the time I was posted in the Higher Education Department. If he felt that I was in the wrong he should have told me so. He had shown himself to be very sympathetic. He was friendly and cordial. We had also spent more than a month together when we had both gone to the Johns Hopkins University in Baltimore, USA for a training programme sponsored by the SIFPSA project and he knew me quite well. I was of course at the time the Director of the Project and he was the Principal Secretary of the Information Department.

I realized. that Shri Yogendra Narain, although he appeared very straight forward and affable but was not quite so. When his remarks were communicated to me, he happened to be posted as the Defence Secretary to the Government of India and I was posted as the Additional Resident Commissioner for UP in Delhi. This was in the year 2003. When I received the letter communicating to me his above remarks, I immediately called him up. He feigned surprise and would not believe that he could have written those comments. He asked me to come and show him the letter. I did that and he asked me to send my representation. The remarks were expunged but again, this entire episode left a bitter taste in my mouth. I appreciate frankness and outspokenness rather than hypocrisy. Also I found this consistently, that the senior officers will always support their peers rather than the junior officers, even though the latter may be right. They will not support a junior officer in his or her fight with a senior officer and so junior officers are very hesitant to voice their views because they know that if they get into a problem nobody will support them.

17

Secretary (Department of Animal Husbandry and Fisheries)

I HAD joined as Secretary of the Department of Animal Husbandry and Fisheries on 1st November 1999. The elections in UP were just over and new ministers were shortly thereafter sworn in. Shri Fagu Chauhan from Azamgarh took over as the Cabinet Minister of the department and Shri Prem Prakash Singh was sworn in as Minister of State. The Animal Husbandry Department was also under the Agricultural Production wing and so policy matters and important files were put up to the minister through the Agricultural Production Commissioner. At this time the Agricultural Production Commissioner was Shri AP Verma of 1966 batch.

It is normally the practice that the Cabinet Minister allots work to the Minister of State. They do not give any important work to their ministers of state. In this case also the Cabinet Minister decided to give Shri Prem Prakash

Singh very perfunctory work relating to unstarred assembly questions, other routine work related to the legislature, matters pertaining to Class III and Class IV employees, training and the 20-point programme of the government.

I had had a brush with Shri Prem Prakash Singh in my earlier stint as Secretary Sericulture too. Shri Prem Prakash Singh was attached to Shri Sardar Singh who was minister for both Sericulture as well as Handlooms. However we soon found out that Shri Prem Prakash Singh was only the Minister of State for Handlooms and not for Sericulture. Anyway he was already being extended all the facilities by the Directorate of Sericulture including vehicles, staff, hospitality on tours and so on even before I joined the department. I began to hear some whispering in the department that Shri Prem Prakash Singh was only Minister of State for Handlooms and not for Sericulture when the departmental vehicle provided to the minister Shri Prem Prakash Singh met with an accident in which it was badly bashed up. He wanted a replacement for this vehicle. The department as normally is the case was short of vehicles. While the matter was being discussed as to how to arrange another vehicle, I got a call from the minister complaining that I had not yet called on him after taking over charge. He also read out to me a long list of transfers he wanted effected. It was then that I decided to check on the rumours that I had heard.

The protocol department confirmed that Shri Prem Prakash Singh was not the Minister of State for Sericulture. The matter was put up to the Cabinet Minister Shri Sardar Singh and he ordered an enquiry as to how Shri Prem

Prakash Singh was being extended all facilities from the department when he had nothing to do with the Department of Sericulture. Shri Prem Prakash Singh's facilities were immediately withdrawn. The Minister of State had obviously taken advantage of the fact that perhaps nobody would have the courage to raise this issue. That was the last I heard of Shri Prem Prakash Singh till I joined as the Secretary of the Department of Animal Husbandry and Fisheries.

In the Department of Animal Husbandry and Fisheries however there was no doubt that Shri Prem Prakash Singh was the Minister of State and as befitting his station and protocol I fixed an appointment to call on him and brief him about the work in the department. This was the first time that I met Shri Prem Prakash Singh. The Minister of State seemed to have a good idea about the working of the department. I came to know that he himself maintained a dairy farm and was a long time contractor for the departmental fish farms particularly in the Terai region. The Irrigation Department had transferred thirteen water bodies to the UP Fisheries Development Corporation for management. Out of these thirteen the fishing contract for two namely, Bhawa and Begul in district Nainital had been secured by Shri Prem Prakash Singh. The contract for these was with Shri Prem Prakash Singh and his family for the last 10 to 15 years with no increase in revenue. Thus for his own personal benefit he had been particularly keen to join this department. He was a contractor for the department he was minister of!

Shri Prem Prakash Singh was extremely frustrated with the Cabinet Minister's work allotment. Looking at matters relating to assembly questions and class 3 and class 4 employees was hardly the work that would cheer him. The work distribution however was the same as that of his predecessor in the previous government. His predecessor however had been Shri Amarmani Tripathi of the Loktantrik Congress who is in jail these days, convicted for the murder of a young pregnant girl Madhumita Shukla. A lot depends upon the personalities of the two ministers and the equation they share. Shri Amarmani Tripathi was a domineering person whereas his Cabinet Minister Shri Gupta was a mild man. This resulted in Shri Amarmani Tripathi running the department and handling all matters which were not officially his concern. He was asking for files unrelated to his work allotment and the files were being sent to him by the then Secretary to the department, Shri Lalit Srivastav of the 1973 batch. The Cabinet Minister's orders about the work distribution remained only on paper. Cabinet Minister Shri Gupta criticized Shri Amarmani Tripathi to his officers but could not say anything to the former face to face. The bureaucrats realized that Shri Amarmani Tripathi was the more powerful of the two and could create problems for them, so they quickly fell in line to do Shri Amarmani Tripathi's bidding.

Shri Prem Prakash Singh obviously got his inspiration from Shri Amarmani Tripathi. He felt that he could continue in the same fashion and that the work distribution was redundant. Shri Prem Prakash Singh, in my very first visit to him, held me responsible for the work distribution. I informed him that the work distribution is the prerogative of the minister and that the Secretary only issues the orders. He however was not convinced. Problems cropped up soon enough. The Minister of State Shri Prem Prakash Singh started asking for tender files, enquiry reports, transfers of senior officers and so on. The matter was brought to the notice of the Cabinet Minister Shri Fagu Chauhan who however was very clear that no unrelated file should go to the Minister of State. The two ministers were not the best of friends and Shri Fagu Chauhan even took adverse note of the fact that officers should go and call on the Minister of State.

The Animal Husbandry Department maintained some State farms for research activities pertaining to dairy, poultry and so on. At the Chak Gajaria farm near Lucknow the department was also maintaining horses for purely breeding purposes. Shri Prem Prakash Singh wanted a horse from the farm for his personal use but as the horses were being maintained for breeding purposes the question did not arise. The minister also had an eye on a tender that was being called for cutting down trees on the Chak Gajaria farm. Bids had already been invited and the last date was over since long back. The matter had reached my office for finalization when suddenly Shri Prem Prakash Singh sent an application from one party namely M/s Jaiswal Timbers, Pilibhit who had not participated in the tender proceedings but was willing to pay much more nearly, ₹ 16 lakh. The Minister of State sent his application with a draft of ₹ 1.6 lakh towards earnest money. This was against all norms and was of course rejected. It also became clear that the tender was being highly undervalued by the forest department in collusion with the Animal Husbandry staff. The tender was rejected and an enquiry was instituted in the matter.

The matter of re-auctioning of the fish farms in Mahoba in district Hamirpur too came up shortly thereafter. This farm had been auctioned 3 years earlier for a paltry sum of ₹ 30,000. The Minister of State began to pressurize us not to hold a fresh auction. The concerned party which held the control of the fish farm had also gone to court to obtain a stay against the impending auction and we were being threatened that if we held the auction we would be committing contempt of court. I went through the papers and the court judgement. There was no stay and so I ordered that the auction be held. On the day fixed for the auction (25 November 1999) the auction could not be held, because the presiding officer of the auction committee, the Joint Development Commissioner of that Division took leave for that day, under pressure I presume. The second time the date for the auction was fixed (7 December 1999), the auction could not take place because the presiding officer had by then been transferred. The third time the date for the auction was fixed, we heard that the District Magistrate had received some instructions from the Chief Minister's office and was not willing to hold the auction. I had to speak to the District Magistrate and to the concerned officer in the Chief Minister's office to impress upon them that the auction must take place as scheduled. Finally the auction did take place and this particular fish farm was auctioned for ₹ 15,20,000 as against the existing ₹ 30,000.

The relationship with Minister of State completely broke down after these episodes. He was not on talking terms with the Cabinet Minister either. Shri Prem Prakash Singh was a history-sheeter and was also involved in a murder case for which he had to make regular appearance in the court at Nainital. My officers had been cautioning me in taking up this fight against Shri Prem Prakash Singh. They said that these people can stoop to any level. Thoroughly frustrated in his designs, he made complaints against me to the Chief Minister and wanted me to be transferred out. The Chief Minister Shri Ram Prakash Gupta asked for the files. The files were sent to the Chief Minister and he was appraised of the situation. Cabinet Minister Shri Fagu Chauhan also explained the matter to the Chief Minister. The Chief Minister was convinced that I was in the right and so he did not oblige Shri Prem Prakash Singh. The Minister of State wrote to the Chief Minister for my transfer three times but to no avail.

Things seemed to have quietened down but suddenly one day on 9th January 2000, on scrutinizing the morning papers I found that all the dailies were carrying front page headlines that the Minister of State Shri Prem Prakash Singh had accused the Secretary Mrs Shankar of corruption and of voluntarily taking decisions which required Cabinet approval and so on. I was stunned. The minister had held a press conference the previous day where he made all these allegations. This was a pre-planned move on the part of the Minister of State when he realized that he had failed to get me transferred. The papers reported that he had said that he would continue to hold these press conferences till Mrs Shankar was transferred out from the department. The Minister of State had also made some derogatory remarks against the Cabinet Minister.

The Cabinet Minister that day happened to be in Azamgarh. I informed him about the situation. He told me not to react and that he would be coming to Lucknow the following week and would hold a press conference himself in addition to talking to the Chief Minister. Two days later while I was making out my report for the Chief Secretary and the Chief Minister, Shri Prem Prakash Singh held a second press conference on 11th January and made further allegations against me. On 13th January he once again held a press conference and this time he made derogatory remarks even against the Chief Minister. He said the Secretary was running the department (which is anyway my work) and that the Cabinet Minister and the Chief Minister were helpless. The paper reported the Minister of State as having commented that if the Chief Minister did not shift me out then even the Chief Minister was hand in glove with the Secretary and that all his talk about his resolve to wipe out corruption was bogus. In Lucknow for full 2 weeks this matter continued to create front page headlines.

Shri Prem Prakash Singh made all sorts of absolutely baseless and wrong allegations against me. His sole aim was to make false allegations against me, confident in the fact that once allegations are made, the damage is done and the onus of fighting them lies on the victim and the accused goes scot-free. Even my steps to improve the functioning of the department which should have been praised were put in a different perspective. Even when I had obtained Cabinet approval he had said that I had not. Even when the Chief Minister reviewed his decision on some issue after a factual note was put up to him, Shri Prem Prakash Singh said that the Secretary openly defies the orders of the Chief Minister and so on and so forth. Nominal increase in the fees for services provided by the department like artificial insemination, sterilization, medical registration etc. was denounced by him as my high-handedness even though it was being done after taking the orders of the empowered sub-committee of the Cabinet and very much required.

In the meantime the Cabinet Minister Shri Fagu Chauhan returned to Lucknow. I met him and asked him about his course of action. He however seemed to have lost his nerve and was not in favour of a press conference. Either he did not want to directly take up cudgels with the Minister of State or there was some pressure on him from the party. It must be mentioned here that the government of the day was a coalition government. When I realized that the Cabinet Minister was hesitant to take a stand, I immediately dispatched my comments on the press cuttings with the request to the Chief Minister that the Minister of State should publicly apologize to me, that the government must issue a press statement that all the allegations made by the Minister of State against me were false and baseless and that I should be given permission to file a case for defamation and damages against the Minister of State at government expense.

I also sent a brief to the Chairman of the UP IAS Officers Association Shri AP Singh, the then Chairman, Board of Revenue. He belonged to the 1964 batch as against his name sake whose reference has come earlier in the book who belonged to 1967 batch. The Association was dilly-dallying with my request to hold a meeting of the executive committee. Shri Harminder Raj Singh of the 1978 batch was the Secretary of the Association at the time and he informed me that the Chairman was not willing to call a meeting. Incidentally both these officers are no more.

Shri AP Singh, Chairman of the Association, would not give me an appointment and it was only after several days of perseverance that I was successful at meeting him. His attitude was most baffling. As soon as I entered the room he said "What is this? I thought you were a good officer, but you create problems everywhere." I was taken aback and explained the whole situation to him. I emphasized the urgency of calling a meeting of the executive committee of the Association. I told him that this was an extremely serious matter and that the Association must take up my matter and support me in fighting the Minister of State. Ministers cannot be allowed to behave in the manner that Shri Prem Prakash Singh had done and get away with it. He would however not agree to calling a meeting of the Association and said that he could talk to Shri Prem Prakash Singh and mediate on my behalf. I told him that I didn't need him to talk to Shri Prem Prakash Singh as that I could do on my own. It was obvious that caste politics was playing a role. Shri AP Singh like Shri Prem Prakash Singh was a Thakur and he believed in being loyal to his caste rather than in discharging his duties independently. I left his room absolutely deflated and disappointed. Finally a small group of officers did meet the Chief Minister and gave him a representation against the Minister of State's behaviour. I too met the Chief Minister again and impressed upon him the need to protect the hard earned reputation of honest officers. The Chief Minister was sympathetic and agreed that the Minister of State was wrong. I also impressed upon him to issue a press statement against the allegations made by the Minister of State as anything that I or the Cabinet Minister said would not carry weight as we were interested parties. If the Chief Secretary or Chief Minister gave a statement, then that would carry weight.

In the meantime my letter to the Chief Minister was taken up by the press and the matter got very good coverage in all the national dailies. *The Indian Express* carried front page headlines—'IAS Lady Officer Says No Minister'. *The Times of India* said—'IAS Officer Not to be Cowed Down by Minister' and so on. Shortly afterwards the Chief Minister during a press conference said "Mrs Shankar is an honest and upright officer." This was front page news in the *Pioneer*. The Chief Minister was also reported to have said that there was a lot of pressure on him to take action against the minister who should mend his ways.

I felt a bit appeased by the above statement of the Chief Minister but felt badly let down by the Cabinet Minister. The struggle was between the Cabinet Minister and Minister of State over work distribution but the Secretary came in between the cross fire. The Cabinet Minister, I felt should have been more aggressive. The Minister of State was by now thoroughly humiliated. The officers of the department realizing that the Minister of State was not in any position to help them stayed away from him. He however continued to write letters asking for files with which he was not concerned, in vain. He was also finally transferred out of the

Department of Animal Husbandry and Fisheries and made Minister of State in the Department of Cooperatives. The minister was further humiliated by the media which provocatively said that the Minister of State had lost the battle against Mrs Shankar and so on. Shri Prem Prakash Singh in another desperate effort once again called a press conference and said that as a lady had been responsible for the downfall of the Kalyan Singh government so also a lady officer would be responsible for the downfall of the Ram Prakash Gupta government.

Soon a large delegation of ministers belonging to Loktantrik Congress, Bahujan Samaj Party, Jantantrik Party, etc, met the Chief Minister and demanded that the Secretary of the department must also be shifted out. Pressure continued to mount. It was a coalition government. The Chief Minister bowed to the pressure and I too was shifted out of the department in April 2000. The Chief Minister Shri Gupta told me categorically that it was a political settlement but that he had told the Chief Secretary that I should be given a good job. Under the circumstances there was nothing more to be done and I handed over the charge of the department.

I got the feeling that Shri Fagu Chauhan, the Cabinet Minister was also happy at my ouster. He had relied very heavily on me in his proxy war against Shri Prem Prakash Singh. However now that he was rid of the latter he felt perhaps that a more pliable Secretary would suit him better. There were several issues on which he would have liked to take a different stand. The minister was keen that the Ex-Director Animal Husbandry Dr AK Singh who had been under suspension even before I joined the department and against whom an enquiry was going on should be reinstated. He told me that he was personally called by Shri Rajnath Singh, the then Minister of Surface Transport, Government of India, at least on three occasions to plead Dr AK Singh's case. Although initially the minister was very keen that this should be done, we had to tell him that this was not possible unless the enquiry report exonerating him was received. Shortly however much to our surprise and comfort the minister changed his tune. Rumours began to float that Dr AK Singh had offered the minister ₹ 35 lakh for his reinstatement. Perhaps this rumour unnerved the minister and he then kept quiet.

Ministers were wary of accepting me as their departmental Secretary after the massive publicity of this episode. I was posted as Secretary, Social Welfare Department but that was immediately changed to Administrator of the Sharda Sahayak Command Area Development Project. This was also cancelled before I could join and I was then kept on compulsory wait, awaiting a posting. Finally the lady minister of the Women's Welfare Department agreed to have me join but by then my husband was transferred to Greater Noida and I decided to ask for a posting near Delhi.

The government did not post me anywhere near Delhi, even though there are so many inane and useless jobs which have been created in Delhi and nearabouts for the express purpose of adjusting officers in and around Delhi. Although for some officers posts are specially created to adjust them, I could not be adjusted with my husband even against any of the available and vacant posts. I continued to be on compulsory wait for a full one year till I joined as Additional Resident Commissioner at New Delhi on 1st May 2001. Shri Ravi Mathur of the 1970 batch was the Resident Commissioner. There was not much work in the Resident Commissioner's office. It basically related to protocol. I got an occasion to meet Shri Rajnath Singh, the then Chief Minister and he graciously agreed to move me out.

18

Additional Chief Executive Officer (NOIDA Authority)

ON 18TH June 2001 orders issued posting me as Additional Chief Executive Officer New Okhla Industrial Development Authority (NOIDA Authority). I was happy that there would at last be some work, and also minimum basic facilities. I got the copy of the order by evening and on 19th June I rang up the Chief Executive Officer of NOIDA Shri VK Malhotra of the 1970 batch, to inform him that I would be joining.

I was surprised when Shri Malhotra did not allow me to join and asked me to wait saying that there was some problem in Lucknow about the transfer chain. Accordingly instead of handing over charge of my post as Additional Resident Commissioner of UP in Delhi in the forenoon I did so in the afternoon so that I could take over on the 20th morning. On the 20th morning however the Chief Executive Officer NOIDA again told me to wait saying that he had got a call from the Industrial Development Commissioner, the infamous Shri AP Singh of the 1967 batch directing the CEO that I should not be allowed to join as my posting orders were being changed. I spoke to the Principal Secretary to the Chief Minister who denied any change and asked me to join. Also when I rang up the Authority in the evening, I was informed that another officer posted as Additional Chief Executive Officer, who too was in the same transfer chain had been allowed to join. It was clear that Shri. AP Singh and Shri VK Malhotra were up to something and so I immediately sent in my joining report. I also sent copies to the Chief Secretary as well as the Appointments Secretary in Lucknow.

Chief Minister Shri Rajnath Singh came to Delhi and I met him on 22nd June and briefed him about the situation. I also showed him the copy of the Industrial Development Commissioner's letter to the CEO which said that Smt Promilla Shankar's orders were being changed and so she should be asked to wait. Shri Rajnath Singh was surprised at Shri AP Singh suo motu issuing orders on his own. He said that he would resolve the issue as soon as he got back to Lucknow that evening. The Chief Minister instructed his Principal Secretary that I should be allowed to join immediately. I got the message but Shri VK Malhotra still did not allow me to join. It was several days later on the 28th of June when the Chief Executive Officer received a letter from the Industrial Development Commissioner Shri AP Singh permitting me to join that I was finally allowed to join. The Industrial Development Commissioner Shri AP Singh had written "In spite of Mrs Shankar's reputation, looking at her seniority she should be allowed to join but that this will not be a hindrance to her imminent transfer." A letter from a man like Shri AP Singh, notorious for corruption and voted as the most corrupt officer in the State of UP by the UP IAS Officers Association making such remarks was strongly repudiated. I lodged my protest against this in writing to the Chief Minister, Chief Secretary and the Appointments Department.

I finally went to office on 2nd July 2001. The whole episode had left a very dirty taste in my mouth. There seemed to be no rule of law. The Industrial Development Commissioner behaved like he was himself the Chief Minister and the Chief Executive Officer of Noida preferred to follow the orders of Shri AP Singh rather than of the Chief Minister. Of the four Additional Chief Executive Officers in the Authority at that time, I was the senior most but I was given very inconsequential work pertaining to law, stores, audit and some limited financial matters. I was sidelined and far removed from the main work in the Development Authority namely the drawing up of the Master Plan, acquisition, development and allotment of land for residential, industrial and commercial purposes, municipal functions of the Authority and so on.

The Law Department of the Authority was heavily involved in legal disputes pertaining to land acquisition, as this was one of the major activities of the Authority. For handling cases on its behalf, the Authority maintained a panel of lawyers and had fixed their rates for different categories of cases. Just before I joined the Authority, Shri AP Singh, Industrial Development Commissioner had ensured that all these files were handed over to only two lawyers namely the

Mishra brothers who were close to him. These two lawyers were based in Allahabad and I was informed that jeep loads of files had been transported to Allahabad overnight to be handed over to them. The Mishra brothers took over the entire work pertaining to appeals in the High Court at Allahabad. But what was highly objectionable was that for the same case both the brothers were being paid separately. Two separate cheques for the same amount were being made out in their two individual names. Moreover the rule in the Authority was that since these cases were small cases they were to be clubbed together so that five cases qualified for making one payment. In the case of the Mishra brothers each case was being paid separately which in effect meant that the outgo was ten times what it should have been. This was grossly irregular to say the least and I put up the matter to the CEO Shri VK Malhotra, who was very unhappy at my raising this issue because he did not want to annoy Shri AP Singh, the mentor of these brothers. He made some inane query and returned the file. His query was answered and the matter was put up to him again for reconsideration. In the meantime while the matter was under consideration I had stopped their payments and had proceeded to Lucknow for a meeting. On my return I was informed that payments had been made to the Mishra brothers at the behest of Shri VK Malhotra in my absence. As the file was still under consideration and the CEO had as yet not recorded his decision, I rang up the bank and advised them not to clear this payment if not already cleared.

Chief Executive Officer was extremely annoyed with me saying that I had disobeyed a senior officer's orders. He sent me a very sarcastic note saying that "ACEO may perhaps be aware that we in the Authority incur an annual expenditure of approximately ₹ 729 crore. It is truly a reflection of the ACEO's brilliance and incisiveness with which a payment of five lakhs approximately has been identified as being worthy of being withheld. Your concern for Authority's petty outgoes such as above has been so touching and indeed admirable that the image of the Authority, disobedience of a senior's order and damage to a professional's dignity have been considered trivial matters. The wonders such a mighty mind can do if it were to concentrate on bigger issues of 729 crores have been really underestimated by us. Orders for better utilization of your strengths in working are therefore being issued separately." Soon the Law Department was withdrawn from my charge.

Another controversial matter pertaining to the legal department was the CEO's orders that the lawyers be paid whatever they asked for. He also began to handle directly some of the sensitive and controversial matters including the file pertaining to the case of Smt Neera Yadav, the Ex-CEO and Chairman of NOIDA Authority against whom serious allegations had been levelled and a CBI enquiry had been instituted.

Finance Department was allocated to me by Shri VK Malhotra for the simple reason that the ACEO's looking after this department were not expected to play any role. It was basically the budget that was put up for discussion once a year. Funds of the Authority had already been deposited in fixed deposits or otherwise in various banks. It was ironic that all payments were sanctioned at the level of the Chief

Accounts Officer. The only matter that came up regularly was the reimbursement of the medical bills of the officers on deputation to the Authority!

Even within the limited scope of work allotted to me I tried to streamline the functioning and bring to the notice of the CEO the ground realities. We started calling for sealed tenders for funds to be deposited. Instead of depositing the money arbitrarily we began depositing the money in the bank that offered us the highest rate of interest. The tendering system was streamlined. Once the tender was final no changes were allowed to be made and the penalty could not be waived off, as was being done at the time. I made efforts to get the ledgers and accounts completed. The Computer Maintenance Corporation (CMC) was doing the work of computerization of the accounts, in the Authority but I found that they had already been paid ₹ 50 lakh certifying that their work had been completed when the work was indeed far from complete. The only work that the staff was interested in was to handle payments so that they could take their commissions. Of the total of 78 account clerks at least 51 were involved only in making payments. I did not find any positive response on any aspect of the functioning of the Authority that I raised with the CEO. I was soon divested of this work also.

As I was looking after Stores, I got the ground water pipes which were being purchased and sent for quality check to the Shriram Institute of Industrial Research. These were also double checked at the IIT (Delhi). Of all the samples which had already been certified by the engineers of the Authority as fit and in uniformity with the standards laid down by the BIS, only one sample adhered to the norms. The others were all found to be sub-standard. These pipes were found containing 50% sulphated ash as against a BIS ceiling of 11%. Unfortunately however most of the pipes had already been laid. A joint survey by the Central and UP Pollution Control Board had described NOIDA's water supply "unfit even for agriculture". I had advised not only the blacklisting of the pipe suppliers but also action against the engineers who had given these firms a clean chit. However the engineer who had brought the matter to my notice was the one against whom action was taken and he was transferred out of the head office.

The verification of the Stores had not taken place since the last ten years. I got the store verification underway. It was brought to my notice that for a particular work PVC pipes of 10 kg/cm^2 pressure were being used, when only 4 or 6 kg/cm^2 pipes were required. When this matter was put up to CEO for rectification no action was taken. The Engineering Department insisted that 10 kg/cm^2 pressure pipes were required but without giving any technical reason for the same. The CEO agreed with the engineering wing and immediately gave orders for purchase. In the meantime we referred the matter to IIT (Delhi) for a technical report in the matter. IIT (Delhi) agreed with the report of the technical examiner who said that only 4 kg/cm^2 pressure pipes were required for the work in question. The Authority was thus incurring wasteful and unnecessary expenditure. As the higher pressure pipes meant more payment it also meant higher commissions.

The last straw on the camel's back came at the time of Diwali. Normally at Diwali the employees of the Authority were given a bonus in the form of some gift. It was the union leaders who would decide what gift was to be given to the employees. It was well-known that the union leaders were interested in purchasing something rather than accepting the bonus in cash as in this way they could negotiate a commission for themselves on the purchases. In the year 2001 the gift that the union leaders decided to purchase was a music system. I spoke to some of the employees and asked them what they thought about the music system. Of course all owned music systems. It was felt that cash would be a much better option as then each employee could buy whatever he needed with the money. All hell broke loose after this recommendation. The union went on strike. The CEO sided with them. I failed to see what was wrong if we paid cash. I thought it was a much better option and the money would be transferred directly into their bank accounts. It would be a hassle free and neat transaction. The union leaders were of course livid because they would not get any commission. As Chairman of the Committee I remained firm that we will not be bullied and brow beaten by a handful of union leaders. I had however failed to anticipate the near revolt on my hands. I was shocked at the resistance to my decision. That petty vested interests can play such havoc so openly was an eye opener. Even a local MLA Shri Nagar joined the fray. However I refused to budge. Finally we did give cash to all the employees and my staff informed me that everyone was happy. Things between me and the CEO had soured irretrievably. We were not even on talking terms and he was trying hard to get me transferred.

A very interesting legal case had come up which reflected the negative attitude of the NOIDA Authority. A scooterist had won a case in the Consumer's Court. The court ordered the Authority to pay the scooterist compensation. The scooterist was riding his scooter one day on one of the main thoroughfares of NOIDA. Two bulls were locked in a battle on the roadside. Suddenly one of the bulls charged at him and gored him very badly. He sustained serious injuries to his spine and was hospitalized for several months. He was lucky to have survived. He won his case in the Consumer Court. He deserved to win as the Authority was at fault. I recommended that we pay the person compensation and at the same time take drastic steps to make NOIDA free of stray animals. The CEO however was in favour of appealing against the decision of the Consumers Court saying that it would otherwise set a very bad precedent. Anyway the main problem was that no one was willing to tackle the matter of stray cattle. The fear of disturbing the status-quo and of annoying anyone is so great that it leads to policy paralysis. Though this work was not in my work distribution, still I called the person looking after health and sanitation in NOIDA, to brief me about what action could be taken. He was most discouraging. They would fall back to mentioning Smt Maneka Gandhi's name and the havoc that she had created when they once tried to capture stray dogs. Thus my efforts to free NOIDA of stray cattle also failed. What kind of modern metros were we developing in which bulls sit on central verges of busy thoroughfares and dairy owners freely take their cattle through them.

The vice like hold of corrupt practices is also clear from the case of compounding fees for construction not in conformity with the Authority's bye-laws. I found that this was only an avenue to make money. If by laws have been made they must necessarily be adhered to. If it is felt that the by-laws need some relaxation they can be amended. But it stands to reason that once the building bye-laws have been finalized they must be followed to the hilt and any construction not in keeping with them must be demolished. There should be no provision for compounding. Loopholes are deliberately left in the Rules and Acts to facilitate corruption. I moved the matter to be put up for a decision in the Board but the file never returned back.

I was finally transferred on 31st January 2002. While I was preparing to leave for office I got a letter from the CEO that I had been relieved from my post in view of my transfer orders. I had not as yet heard about or received my transfer orders but the CEO in a desperate hurry to see the last of me relieved me. It is every officer's right to hand over charge properly, tie up the loose ends and take one's personal papers and belongings from the office. So in spite of the CEO's orders I went to office and conducted my matters in a routine way. The next day however the CEO got my room locked and my name plate removed. My staff rang up to inform me of the situation. Under the circumstances I did not go to office but decided to get the transfer orders stayed and to leave on my own terms.

Elections were due shortly and the model code of conduct was in force. I spoke to the Appointment Secretary Shri Hari Paliwal of the 1982 batch and the Industrial Development Commissioner who was by now Shri SN Shukla of the 1967 batch. They took up my case with the Chief Secretary. In the meantime my batch mate Shri Sayan Chatterjee who was in the Central Election Commission also spoke to the Chief

Electoral Officer of UP Shri Noor Mohammad to stay my transfer order till the elections were over. The Chief Executive Officer visited the Election Commission and tried his best that my order should not be stayed. He met Shri Lyngdoh, the Chief Election Commissioner. However no one was convinced and soon the Election Commission advised the Chief Electoral Officer to get my transfer order stayed till the election procedure was completed. The State Government issued orders accordingly. The Authority however did not send me a copy of the order so I rang up my staff and informed them that I would be coming to take over charge and that they should inform the CEO's office that if my room was not opened I had no option but to get the lock broken. I also informed the Appointments Secretary of my course of action and told him to inform the Chief Secretary also. The CEO was told to follow the orders of the government and see to it that the reputation of the government is not discredited. Anyway not taking anything for granted I took with me an ironsmith just in case I found the room still locked. The need however did not arise. The room had been opened and cleaned. My name plate was in place. My staff welcomed me.

I had as expected no work. I only pursued matters which the Chairman Shri SN Shukla asked me to do. The Chairman and CEO too were not getting along. The CEO was openly defying the Chairman. On being advised by the Chairman to call a meeting of the Board, the CEO would not do so. When the Chairman suggested that the Board meeting be called on 13th February the CEO wanted the meeting called in the 2nd week of March. The Chairman again told him that the meeting be called on 13th February but when CEO failed to send notice the Chairman suo motu on his own called the meeting on 25th February. The CEO did not attend the Board meeting. The Chairman then asked the CEO to call a meeting again either on 22nd March or 27th March. The CEO took no action on this and again the Chairman at his own level issued a notice for the meeting on 27th March. There were very important issues that needed to be discussed in the meeting. The Board was to be informed about some serious financial irregularities. Rumours were rife. Things were getting out of hand. The Authority was cutting a very sorry figure. Finally the government taking cognizance of what was happening in the NOIDA Authority transferred both Shri SN Shukla and Shri VK Malhotra. Shri SN Shukla was immediately relieved from his charge while the government waited for the CEO to hand over charge. I on my part waited for the polling process to be over and without waiting for the counting, handed over charge and took over as Additional Resident Commissioner of UP at Delhi on 25th February 2002.

CEO Shri VK Malhotra stooped to very low levels. He was not on good terms even with Shri Shukla's predecessor Smt Sumita Kandpal. He showed scant regard for her and when Smt Kandpal retired in September 2001, she was not given a farewell. Not only that, he was not even there to see her off. Smt Kandpal retired and left the office where she had been Chairman for more than five years, seen off to her car only by her personal staff.

NOIDA is a thoroughly corrupt organization. Most of the staff had vested interests. Many of them were working as property agents. Even my peon I was informed came to office in a car. His land had been acquired by the Authority and he had received handsome compensation. This organization has been used by successive governments as milch cattle. Wherever you put a finger in that organisation, you will find rot underneath.

Due to the rampant corruption every engineer and officer is a crorepati. Nothing gets done in routine. Money has to change hands. Only a corrupt officer can carry on here. Honest officers will firstly not get posted here and if posted cannot last for even a month, unless given no work at all. There have been all sorts of scams in recruitment, promotions, land allottments and acquitions, tenders, practically in each and every sphere, but no action has been taken against anyone.

Things in the organization I heard kept going from bad to worse under successive governments. Orders were taken directly from the Chief Minister's office with no respect for rules and regulations. All allotments, tenders, recruitments, etc, were cleared by the Chief Minister's office.

19

Commissioner (NCR UP Ghaziabad–I)

I HAVE had serious problems whenever Ms Mayawati has come to power in UP. As soon as she came to power in 2002, I was shifted from the post of Additional Resident Commissioner at New Delhi and posted as Secretary, Department of Banking in Lucknow. I joined in Lucknow and proceeded on leave. Finally I was once again adjusted in the post of Additional Resident Commissioner New Delhi where I took over on 4th July 2002.

Shri Ajit Seth of the 1974 batch currently the Cabinet Secretary in the Government of India was at that time the Resident Commissioner for UP. There were too many officers in the Resident Commissioner's office and consequently there were neither rooms for their accommodation nor vehicles for their use available for allotment. Even officers posted in Lucknow and handling important departments were given additional charge of the post of Additional Resident Commissioners. Shri Ajit Seth created a lot of complications because he refused to issue any order as to how the rooms or vehicles were to be shared but left it to the officers to settle their own matters. He was always on the run from the office making a brief appearance at some time of the day and just as quickly doing the vanishing act. I was the senior most Additional Resident Commissioner and asked him to issue some order but to no avail. Soon I was posted as Commissioner, NCR Planning Cell, UP. I took over charge on 18th December 2002 but in a matter of 10 days I was again shifted out to Lucknow. I handed over the charge of the post of Commissioner NCR on 31st December 2002.

I joined in Lucknow as Secretary, Agricultural Industries and Agricultural Export Promotion. My husband was posted in Delhi, my children were also there but the government would not adjust me there. I would also like to mention here that none of the jobs I was holding at this time were of any consequence and so did not warrant any shift. I remained on earned leave for a period of 6 months. While I was on leave I requested Shri PL Punia, an officer of the 1971 batch, at that time Principal Secretary to Ms Mayawati to transfer me near Delhi and even to let me know the reason for my constant harassment. Shri Punia is now Congress MP (Rajya Sabha) and Chairman of the National Commission for Scheduled Castes. I even entreated Shri DS Bagga (1967 batch), the then Chief Secretary to transfer me anywhere near Delhi. They kept assuring me that something will be done, agreeing that it was rather unfair on me. However, I soon realized that it was a futile effort. I did not even know the reason why I was being troubled and so finally proceeded on one year's study leave. I was on study leave from 8th June 2003 to 7th June 2004. My topic for study was 'Motivation in the Civil Services' which I felt was non-existent.

Some years later Shri Punia told me that it was Shri Bagga the then Chief Secretary who was responsible for my discomfiture, that the Chief Secretary would sit in the afternoons with the Chief Minister and fill her ears with gossip. On the other hand Shri DS Bagga who subsequently also fell out with Ms Mayawati and had a tough time himself, told me that it was Shri Punia who had created problems for me. I don't know whom to believe and what to believe.

By the time I joined back from study leave the government had changed and the Samajwadi Party was in power. The government acceded to my request for a posting near Delhi and I once again took over as Additional Resident Commissioner in Delhi on 23rd June 2004. On 18th August 2004, I was transferred as Chief Investment Commissioner for UP at New Delhi itself. I took over from Shri CK Sharma, an officer of 1971 batch. Shri Sharma had left without paying back a couple of lakhs outstanding against his name on account of travelling advance. We had a tough time getting him to clear his advances. Nevertheless after a year Shri CK Sharma managed to oust me from the post. On 28th October 2005 I took over as the Chief Executive Officer of the Taj Expressway Authority. There was no work on this job as the work had come to a standstill after the Samajwadi Party stopped the clearances of Jaypee Associates because the clearances had been given to them by the BSP government earlier. I was soon transferred once again and on 22nd May 2006 I took over as Commissioner, NCR for UP at Ghaziabad, where I continued till 30th June 2007 when Ms Mayawati once again became the Chief Minister and transferred me to Lucknow. Once again I had no option but to be on leave. I was not in a position to join in Lucknow.

My husband was in Delhi, my daughter too was here and I was busy arranging her marriage. My mother was unwell and expired soon thereafter in October 2007 and my father needed looking after. I continued to be on leave from July 2007 to February 2009. I exhausted my commuted leave, my earned leave and for eight months I was on extraordinary leave without pay when I realized that the government had no intention of posting me and five years which was the tenure of the present government, was too long a period to be on leave.

My husband was on deputation with the Government of India but I could not get a posting in Government of India because I was not empanelled due to my less than outstanding Annual Confidential Reports. As all readers would know by now, I have had a chequered career in the service and had decided that it was better to feel free and easy in mind rather than to be all the time under tension to keep the boss happy. I had mentally reconciled myself to the idea that I would not be empanelled. You cannot become empanelled unless you have all outstanding reports. I felt that it was much better to speak one's mind rather than be pressurized to keep saying yes sir even when you disagree with the decision. For me the freedom to speak my mind and write what I want is of extreme importance.

Initially I kept representing to the government but to no avail. I was told that the Cabinet Secretary of UP Shri Shashank Shekhar Singh was the one responsible for my troubles this time. Even when the Chief Secretary Shri Prashant Mishra of the 1972 batch put up a proposal for my adjustment, he would not put up the file to the Chief

Minister. The Chief Secretary was reduced to a mere rubber stamp. All files were to be put up to the Chief Minister by the Chief Secretary through the Cabinet Secretary. Shri SS Singh was obviously livid at my taking up the issue of him making inroads into the service and consequently tried to create as many problems as he could for me. Ms Mayawati on her part would not meet anyone. She had given written instructions that she would not meet officers and that all administrative matters were to be looked after by Shri Shashank Shekhar Singh. I did manage to get an opportunity to meet her in Delhi for the first time on her birthday. She sat in a small room in a courtyard at the back of the house. There was only one chair on which she sat. One had to remove one's footwear to enter her august presence. I stood in front of her for barely a minute. I got the impression that she did not know me which proved to me that she was going wholly by the recommendations of her advisors not knowing anything.

Shri Shashank Shekhar Singh was also behind the pressure on me to vacate the official residence of the NOIDA Authority that I was occupying at the time. As a government servant I was entitled to that residence. My predecessors were also staying in the official residences provided to them by the NOIDA Authority as these offices had no residences of their own. Moreover officers working in Lucknow whose families required to stay in Delhi for personal reasons were designated as Additional Resident Commissioners, Delhi or Officers on Special Duty in addition to their substantive charge at Lucknow so that they could be allotted a house by the NOIDA Authority and their families could stay there.

While I was entitled to the house and unfairly asked to vacate the house, at the same time the wife of an IAS officer Shri RP Singh of the 1982 batch, who was at the time working in Patna as OSD to Shri Nitish Kumar, former Chief Minister of Bihar was allotted a house by the NOIDA Authority. She had absolutely no business to be occupying a house of the Authority. She was not even employed. When I raised this matter that here, I was an officer of the cadre entitled to a house but being whimsically and unfairly forced to vacate, there was this lady whose husband had already left NOIDA some years back and then had left UP itself on deputation to Bihar being allotted a house, I was told that her case was different because Shri Nitish Kumar had personally spoken to Ms Mayawati. This is the unfairness and injustice that one experiences in UP. If one has the right connections one can get anything done but if one is not politically connected they can stoop to any level to harass you.

20

Commissioner (NCR UP Ghaziabad–II)

THE FINAL blow to my career came just before my retirement. I joined as Commissioner, National Capital Region Planning Cell, UP on 6th January 2011. The office was based in Ghaziabad. There was not too much pressure of work and after eight months when my retirement was just 6 months away and I had begun to fill in my pension papers, the government dropped a bombshell. On 9th September 2011 the Chief Minister Sushree Mayawati of the Bahujan Samaj Party placed me undeı suspension. The reason given was that I had proceeded on two days causal leave to Colombo on a private visit informing the government but not awaiting the government's sanction letter. This came as a great shock. I could never in my dreams have foreseen that one day I will be placed under suspension. Suspension of an officer is to be resorted to when he or she commits an act, the punishment for which would normally result in removal or dismissal from service.

The prime responsibility of the Commissioner, NCR Planning Cell, is the proper planning of the NCR area. The

Cell prepares the Sub-Regional Plan. The Master Plans of the Development Authorities in this area have to be in conformity with the Regional Plan prepared by the NCR Planning Board, Government of India. This plan is prepared for a period of 20 years and is approved by the Board chaired by the Minister of Urban Development, Government of India and members include the Chief Ministers of Delhi, UP, Haryana and Rajasthan. These Chief Ministers have several districts in their State constituting the NCR. The Sub-Regional Plan is prepared by the constituent States in conformity with the norms laid down in the Regional Plan and similarly the Master Plans of the various Development Authorities falling within that sub-region have to be in conformity with the Regional Plan and the Sub-Regional Plan. Metro centres of more than 10 lakh population and regional centres in the range of 3-10 lakhs population can be identified only in the Regional Plan. NCR Planning Cell when it formulates the Sub-Regional Plan can also identify centres namely sub-regional centres, central villages and basic villages but only those of less than 3 lakh population.

In spite of the key role envisaged for the NCR Board of the State Government in the regional planning of the area by the Government of India, the UP Government has always given short shrift to the NCR. It is a post which is considered inconsequential. Many officers of the Development Authorities do not know what the work of the NCR Cell is. The State Government has not found it fit to nominate a member of the NCR Cell on the boards of these Authorities. These Authorities bypass the NCR Cell very frequently and send matters only where they want to shirk responsibility. Information asked by the Cell is not forthcoming, meetings called by the Commissioner are either unattended or attended by very junior officers. The CEOs and Chairmen of these authorities are more often than not junior to the Commissioner NCR but they neither call on them nor take their calls, not attend their meetings. These officers think they are a league apart, available only to the Chief Minister. During the time I was Commissioner NCR, I also happened to be the senior most officer of the State.

The development authorities in this area namely those of NOIDA, Greater NOIDA, Ghaziabad, Baghpat, Meerut, Bulandshahr and the Yamuna Expressway have traditionally been looked upon as milch cows. Corruption was rampant here. Postings in these authorities are extremely coveted jobs for those who want to make money. Here even the clerks and peons are very wealthy and many of them are involved in property dealings. The government of the day would always take keen interest and be fully involved in the activities of these Development Authorities.

In her earlier stint as Chief Minister Ms Mayawati's modus operandi was a little different. There were two stories which were doing the rounds. One concerned a District Magistrate of Ghaziabad. It was said that as he was a Scheduled Caste officer he was quite close to Ms Mayawati and had obviously got the much coveted posting of DM Ghaziabad because of her. The District Magistrate was alleged to have made a beautiful house in Ghaziabad for himself but was foolish enough to invite Ms Mayawati to the house warming party. Ms Mayawati came and looked around obviously impressed. She told the District Magistrate that this house would be suitable for her sister. That was the last that the District Magistrate saw of his own house and must have spent agonizing hours over its loss. Another story we heard was concerning an officer in Lucknow who was asked if it was true that he had a large plot in NOIDA. He is said to have confirmed the fact that he did but it was a small little place. When asked about its value he gave a low figure and then the bombshell was dropped. Ms Mayawati would buy that plot at a slightly higher price. The officer could not have imagined even in his wildest dreams that he will be divested of his plot in this fashion.

One day one of my officers Shri AK Tyagi, Assistant Planner who was also holding charge of the post of Chief Coordinator Planner told me that he had been summoned to Lucknow for a meeting by the Secretary Housing. Although there was no communication to me as head of the office nor any agenda, I allowed him to attend the meeting. A few days later however he again informed me that the Secretary Housing had once more summoned him to Lucknow. Shri Alok Kumar, Secretary (Housing) was a comparatively junior officer belonging to the 1988 batch. Protocol provides that when you want the participation of an organization you inform the head of the office and also send the agenda of the meeting. Here I was being kept totally in the dark and my officers were being summoned to Lucknow as though they were not working with me but were directly working with the department at Lucknow. When Shri Tyagi informed the Secretary that he would have to send a communication in writing to the Commissioner, I was informed that Shri Alok Kumar had thrown a fit saying that nobody is above the government. As mentioned earlier, officers in the Secretariat of UP, consider the subordinate offices as their personal offices to be ordered around. I was anyway insistent and only on receiving a written communication, I allowed my officer to attend the meeting in Lucknow. Instead of one day he had to stay there for 3 days.

On his return he informed me that the master plan of the Yamuna Expressway Authority 2031 was being formulated in Lucknow. He seemed to be under severe stress. The Authority was preparing a master plan for a population of 35 lakhs which was totally unrealistic. When he had expressed his misgivings about this plan he was presented before the Cabinet Secretary Shri Shashank Shekhar Singh. It was Shri Shashank Shekhar Singh who was running the government and senior IAS officers I was told stood, bowed and listened to him, scared to utter a word. He had a reputation also of being very abusive. Shri Tyagi told me that he could not say anything as he was a junior officer and all the senior IAS officers including Shri Ravinder Singh, Additional Cabinet Secretary and Principal Secretary (Housing), Shri VN Garg, Industrial Development Commissioner, Shri Mohinder Singh, Chairman and CEO of Yamuna Expressway Authority were present and nobody said a word. The Cabinet Secretary ordered him to prepare the master plan within two hours! This matter was to come up for the approval of the Board of the Yamuna Expressway Authority on the 2nd of September 2011 and they were all keen that it should be finalized in that meeting. Before the matter could get further complicated, I decided to write to all concerned including the Cabinet Secretary and the Chief Secretary that the NCR Planning Cell would not be able to include the proposed master plan of

Yamuna Expressway Authority in the Sub-Regional plan as it was not in conformity with the Regional plan.

This master plan of the Yamuna Expressway Authority envisaging a population of 35 lakhs was a total and gross violation of the regional plan 2021. It was also absolutely unrealistic.

The Yamuna Expressway Authority had not followed the density norms of urbanization laid down in the Regional Plan. This determined the density norms at 150-200 persons per hectare but the Yamuna Expressway Authority was working on the norm of around 50 persons per hectare. Density norms determine the area to be planned for development. Thus the lesser the density the more the land that requires to be acquired. Even the Planning Commission's steering committee had recommended that we must go vertically not horizontally for more affordable housing in the NCR area. Moreover the Yamuna Expressway Authority area had been earmarked in the Regional plan 2021 as Agricultural Rural Zone outside the Controlled Area and there can be no urbanization in these areas.

The most serious provision was that pertaining to the proposal of 35 lakhs population by 2031. The entire 584 sq kms area (out of a total of 2,689 sq kms) of the Yamuna Expressway Authority which falls within the NCR was to be urbanised. This area comprises part of Gautam Budh Nagar and Bulandshahr district. Moreover according to the 2011 census the population of NOIDA which was set-up in 1976 is 7 lakhs after induced development while the ultimate population for NOIDA is envisioned at 25 lakhs for 2031. Similarly the population of Greater NOIDA which was set-up in 1987 is not more than 1 lakh according to the 2011 census though it is much closer to Delhi than the Yamuna Expressway area. In the last 35 years, in spite of its close proximity to Delhi, NOIDA has been able to attract only a population of 7 lakhs. Under the circumstances it was inconceivable how the Yamuna Expressway Authority could garner a population of 35 lakhs in 20 years given its inherent limitations as compared to the other two Authorities. Moreover these two towns are far from saturated, hence there was no need for further urbanization in the area.

I did not see how the management of Yamuna Expressway Authority and the Government of UP could come up with the proposal of 35 lakhs in a period of 20 years. This was obviously being done for changing the land use and making allotments with mala fide intentions. The Authority had gone ahead with acquiring land under emergency clauses and allotting it to the builders without the master plan having been approved. In a short period the Yamuna Expressway Authority allotted 22,000 plots, a figure which is much larger than the total number of plots allotted in Greater NOIDA till date. Possession of the land was also being handed over to the builders on their depositing just 10% of the total cost of the land and the rest was to be recovered from them in easy instalments over a period of a few years. As rumours went a large amount of money was being taken under the table for allotment and so the builders did not have the money to make the full payment. In the case of NOIDA and Greater NOIDA there was a further moratorium of two years. While this generous policy was in place for the builders, the private individuals who delayed their payments to the Authority had to pay very high interest rates, as much as 18% even for a delay of a few days. Acquisition of land was making farmers jobless and helping to create social unrest. It was very obvious that both the officers of the Authority and the officers in the government were colluding with the land mafia in acquiring large tracts of land for profiteering.

The NCR Planning Board Act 1985 lays down that nothing in the Sub-Regional Plan can be inconsistent with the Regional Plan. Section 27 of the Act says, "The provisions of this Act shall have effect not withstanding anything inconsistent there with contained in any other law for the time being in force or in any instruments having effect by virtue of any law other than this act or in any decree or order of any court or tribunal or other authority." Section 29(i) of the Act also says—"On and from the coming into operation of the finally published Regional Plan, no development shall be made in the region which is inconsistent with the Regional Plan as finally published." The Regional Plan 2021 in para 1.3.2 affirms the legality of the plan by quoting the remarks of the Honourable Supreme Court dated 31st March 1994 saying—"The overriding effect of the act by virtue of section 27 and total prohibition of any activity of development in violation of the finally published Regional Plan provided in section 29 of the Act is sufficient to indicate that any claim inconsistent with the finally published Regional Plan in the area cannot be sustained on any ground."

I would like to mention here that a previous matter where the Yamuna Expressway Authority had proposed a population of 7 lakhs was already sent to the NCR Planning Board in the year 2009 but the NCR Planning Board,

Government of India had not given its approval even for that, obviously because it was not in conformity with the Regional Plan 2021.

Keeping all these points in view a detailed letter setting forth the status and legal standing of the proposed master plan was sent to the Cabinet Secretary Shri Shashank Shekhar Singh, Chief Secretary Shri Anoop Mishra, Industrial Development Commissioner Shri VN Garg, Secretary Housing and Urban Development Shri Alok Kumar and Chairman and CEO Yamuna Expressway Authority Shri Mohinder Singh. The letter was dispatched on 1st September 2011 by fax. Shri AK Tyagi was also sent with a copy to the meeting of the Yamuna Expressway Authority Board which was held on the 2nd September 2011. The draft master plan could not be approved in that meeting in view of my letter mentioned above.

Around the same time I sent a letter to the government informing them that I would be availing of 2 days casual leave on the 5th and 6th of September in order to visit Colombo with my husband. Government response as we know is very tardy. Neither does a response come from the government nor is it expected. It was my duty to inform them which I did and then I proceeded to Colombo. On my return, I was placed under suspension for availing of this leave without awaiting a formal sanction, the rejection of which was never issued or received. I was placed under suspension vide the government's letter dated 9th September 2011. My letter against the Master Plan obviously stunned them into finding themselves handicapped in going ahead with the intended scam. Time was also of the essence as they wanted to finalize the matter before the elections in February 2012. They must have spent considerable time in deciding how they could punish me. Finding no ground against me they could only take recourse to this matter of leave which would have been received in the government around the same time.

Another reason to place me under suspension about which I was informed repeatedly by some officers was that I had now become the senior most officer in the State, by virtue of which I was to be nominated as the president of the UP IAS Officers Association. The Association was lying defunct and during the time of Ms Mayawati and Shri Shashank Shekhar Singh, in five years not one meeting had been held as these two people had completely muzzled the Association. Every officer was afraid to raise his or her voice. UP has a long tradition of a week-long gala festival known as the 'Service Week' where all IAS officers of the State attend. Besides some conferences there are lunches and dinners with the Chief Minister and the Governor. The fact that I was to take over as the President of the Association would have definitely given jitters to Shri Shashank Shekhar Singh who would have expected me to mobilize the officers against him. This could also have been the reason why I was placed under suspension because the purpose as far as the Yamuna Expressway plan was concerned could have been served much better by simply transferring me. I would like to mention here that the Secretary of the UP IAS Officers Association Shri Sanjay Bhoosa Reddy who is also today the Secretary of the All India IAS Officers Association did not get in touch with me while there was time but got in touch with me when I had hardly a few days to go before my retirement. The Association in UP was defunct and office bearers looked upon it as a mere bargaining ground for themselves.

I was the senior most officer in UP. Even the Chief Secretary was two batches junior to me. I didn't need anybody's permission for availing two days casual leave. Moreover Government of India's orders issued in 2007 clearly state that officers do not need permission to go abroad on purely private visits. I was aware that being the senior most officer did not qualify me as a candidate for the post of Chief Secretary because the governments of the day being what they are, want pliable and obedient civil servants at the helm of affairs. They want officers who will facilitate them in their vested interests rather than those who create hindrances. A person like me who has never hesitated to speak her mind is an anathema for the political class but to be placed under suspension for no rhyme or reason was of course another matter. This was a bolt from the blue for me. I have always upheld what I thought was right without any regard for the consequences to myself. I never thought that at the very fag end of my career I will be rewarded in this fashion by a thoroughly corrupt government. One can only be placed under suspension for a misdemeanour which will warrant a punishment as severe as dismissal from service, removal or compulsory retirement from the service. Availing of two days casual leave was no reason.

Knowing that the Government of UP had deliberately taken this step to humiliate and harass me and bring me to my knees, I appealed to the Government of India as provided for in the Service Rules. My first letter to the Government of India was dated 4th October 2011. The letter was sent to

Smt Alka Sirohi, Secretary (Personnel) (MP, 1974) with copies to the Cabinet Secretary and Principal Secretary to the Prime Minister. On pursuing the matter, I was told that the Personnel Department did not move this matter because the word appeal and the relevant section under which I was representing was not mentioned in my letter. On learning this I sent another letter mentioning the word 'appeal' and the relevant section on 14th November 2011! The matter finally moved thereafter in January 2012. The Secretary, Department of Personnel Smt Alka Sirohi of the 1974 batch was least helpful. She would not take my calls. One day I called her five times and left a message on her mobile but there was no response. When I tried to contact her on the landline, I would get the message that she would call later but, of course, she never did. Shri Ajit Seth the Cabinet Secretary who belongs to 1974 batch of the UP cadre was an officer with whom I had worked earlier but he too never took my calls. Whenever I called I would get the standard response that he was not in office and you may please leave your contact number. I left message any number of times but I never got a return call. This is the kind of helpfulness and sensitivity they showed! It was only Shri Pulok Chatterjee, Principal Secretary to the Prime Minister, an officer of the UP cadre belonging to 1974 batch, who had the courtesy to return my call.

Most of the officers were unhelpful and insensitive. The one and only person I met personally on the advice of my friends and colleagues was Shri Narayanasamy, Minister of State, Department of Personnel, but he instead of expediting the matter appeared to have ensured that the matter dragged on still further by referring it to the Department of Law even when there was no legal point involved. The Law Department too sat on the file for a month in spite of the most determined follow up. The file went up and down with some query or the other. Finally I read in the newspaper that the Law Department had noted on the file that "keeping in view my impending retirement a lenient view may be taken in the matter." This was surely not legal analysis! There was nothing on the merits of the case. The orders for my reinstatement finally issued on 16th February 2012 barely two weeks before my retirement. A matter that should have taken not more than a month, took six months to be settled. My suspension was declared void ab initio. Anyway this was the first instance of its kind where the Government of India had stepped in to revoke a suspension order passed by a State Government. I reassumed the charge of Commissioner (NCR) from the very next day that is 17th February 2012. The news of my reinstatement by the Government of India was flashed in detail by all the local papers.

The State Government had sent me a charge-sheet asking for a reply within fifteen days. I sent my reply to the charge-sheet in time but shortly afterwards I received a letter from the State Government calling for my explanation as to why I had still not sent my reply. On making enquiries I found that the State Government had refused to accept the couriered letter and had returned it. The courier service also did not inform me. This was the second time an incident like this had happened. Another letter couriered by me had also not been accepted. After the rebuttal of the charge-sheet the State Government then set-up a two member committee to enquire and report in the matter. After the completion of 90 days the State Government issued a fresh order placing me under suspension for a further period of three months extending beyond my date of retirement!

After my suspension, charge of Commissioner had been given to Shri Chob Singh Verma, a Provincial Civil Service officer promoted to the 1996 batch of IAS. He was to retire at the end of January 2012. He was sent as Commissioner with the express purpose of facilitating the clearance of the master plan of the Yamuna Expressway Authority. He did his best to satisfy the government complaining that Shri Tyagi was not willing to toe the line and was creating problems. This resulted in Shri Tyagi's transfer to the other extreme end of the State namely district Azamgarh in eastern UP. Shri Chob Singh Verma on retirement in January 2012 was rewarded by a post retirement job. He was posted as Member of the State Public Services Tribunal.

The charge of the Commissioner's office was subsequently given to Shri Bhuvanesh Kumar an officer of 1995 batch who was holding charge as Commissioner of the Meerut Division. He was to hold additional charge of the post of Commissioner NCR. On joining office I got my Personal Secretary to inform Shri Bhuvanesh Kumar that I was reassuming my duties and if he wished he could speak to me. He did not. I was briefed about what had transpired after my leaving the office six months back. I found that the Sub-Regional plan was prepared in a months' time at Lucknow and sent to Government of India. The charge of the post of Chief Coordinator Planner was given to Shri NR Verma, Chief Town and Country Planner for UP at Lucknow and Shri Tyagi's job was given to a town planner in the Ghaziabad Development Authority. The entire exercise of making the Sub-Regional plan was done sitting at Lucknow. My orders had been reversed. Shortcuts were taken and the procedures were not followed. The extremely important step in making any master plan which is the calling of objections from the public was done away with. This was an extremely serious lapse but the State Government was in a great hurry to finalize the plan before the elections.

Elections in Ghaziabad were to be held on 28th February 2012. The entire staff was to be deployed on election duty which in effect meant that they would have to leave for their polling stations on 26th or 27th. 29th too would also be a holiday as the next day after the elections is declared a holiday. I anyway did not have much time in office. After two days in the office I began to hear rumours about my transfer to Lucknow and was even accosted by journalists about my future course of action. I had received no transfer orders but shortly thereafter one day the official driver arrived very early in the morning and said that Shri Bhuvanesh Kumar, Commissioner, Meerut, had asked for the vehicle immediately and on his failing to do that had threatened him with an FIR and arrest. Soon thereafter my Personal Secretary also rang up to say that she was threatened with an FIR if she got the Commissioner's room opened for me and that under the circumstances she had decided to resign and would not be attending office. There was a total vacuum in the office. The charge of the various posts in the office were held by officers in other places. The staff was waiting and watching. On the 24th February I received my transfer orders that I was being shifted to Lucknow as the Chairman of the Administrative Tribunal No

II. The next two days that is 25th and 26th were holidays. On 27th the staff would be leaving for poll duty. 28th was the polling and 29th would be a holiday for all those who were engaged in the polling work. On 29th I would be signing my retirement papers. My work suddenly came to an abrupt halt.

I took up the matter of my transfer to Lucknow for just a few days with the Chief Election Commissioner. The elections were on and the model code of conduct was in force. In response to my representation against my transfer the Election Commission on 26th February issued orders posting me as a special observer for the elections in Gautam Budh Nagar. This meant that I would not be joining in Lucknow but as far as the Commissioner's office was concerned the State Government by its cheap tactics had vitiated the atmosphere so much that even a PS or a peon was not available to me. This was done deliberately.

On 29th February 2012, the day of my superannuation, there was nobody in the office in Ghaziabad. I signed the charge certificate and faxed it to Lucknow from my husband's office in Delhi and thus in this abominable and humiliating manner my career spanning 36 years came to an end. On 1st March 2012 at 1.30 PM I got the UP Government's letter that although the Government of India had declared my suspension void ab initio the enquiry would continue. Incidentally the enquiry report of the committee which had been set-up by the State Government had already submitted the report which absolved me totally, to the Appointments Department on 1st February 2012 itself.

Election results were announced on 6th March 2012. Of the 403 Assembly seats, Ms Mayawati could win only 98. The

Samajwadi Party won 220 seats. There was a clear mandate for a change of guard at the helm of affairs. On 15th March 2012 Shri Akhilesh Yadav was sworn in as Chief Minister.

After retirement from government service and after my pending matters and dues were settled, I got associated with an NGO—Resolving to Transform India Foundation. In December 2012, I filed a public interest petition, a Writ under Article 32 of the Constitution seeking issuance of a Writ of Mandamus or any other Writ, directing the respondents to take urgent steps to safeguard women and children across the country who are victims of rape and molestation. I had requested the Honourable Supreme Court to suspend the membership and the privileges of the tainted members of Parliament and the State legislatures who are charge-sheeted for rape and murder and their trial to be done in fast track courts, to cancel the bail of offenders, to suspend tainted police and government officials who are charge-sheeted for rape, to remove VIP security from all except constitutional authorities so that the police force is available for the safety and security of the general public. Certain other similar issues have also been taken up and an open letter was sent to the Chief Justice of India when the police was dragging its feet over the lodging of an FIR against Justice AK Ganguly who had allegedly misbehaved with his young intern.

PART II

LESSONS LEARNT

WE ALL rue the lack of governance in the country. My narration reinforces the way bureaucrats and politicians indulge in petty politicking rather than thinking of the broader issues of growth and progress, relegating governance to the background. Governance in my view basically means to act according to rules and regulations in a quick and prompt manner and to punish the law breakers swiftly, without fear or favour. There has to be zero tolerance for breaking rules and a total disregard for any extraneous factor. It is not a difficult task but nepotism, favouritism, vested interest, fear and corruption have made the system unworkable. It is these tendencies that have to be curtailed immediately to improve the system. Every citizen must feel confident that justice and the rule of law will prevail and also that law breakers will be brought to book.

The problems the country is facing are manifold. Every sector has similar serious problems of governance. My experiences in UP would have given a good idea as to the difficult circumstances under which an honest and independent-minded officer has to work. It is very obvious that they find it extremely difficult to make a difference and take far reaching decisions. They find themselves caught in petty inane matters. The situation may only be marginally different in other States.

In the following pages my attempt is to highlight some of the more serious problems that UP in particular and the country in general are facing today. How far can we go in solving these problems, however is a very big question. Political parties so far have shown us only a very narrow self-serving objective to perpetuate themselves in power at any cost, however damaging it may be to the society. They engage in divisive and sectarian politics and in the process destroy the very fabric of good governance. Experience has shown that we cannot expect them to take any decision which is in the bigger interest of the country. The bureaucrats have fallen in line or are at best indifferent and there are hardly any bureaucrats today who can stand up to the politicians with total disregard to their career graph. Doing well in service and getting important and so-called coveted jobs is what matters to them.

The need of the hour in my opinion is the upliftment of our national character. Governance is an inclusive phenomenon. Even if the government of the day improves, its role can only be limited. Both the government and the people in tandem only can improve governance. If we have to progress we have to work towards a disciplined society. Our children should be taught to be good, honest and disciplined citizens. They should be brought up to be law abiders and not law breakers. We must inculcate in them a very strong sense of patriotism. This can only be done by improving our system of education and also by ensuring that we recruit the best people as far as strength of character is concerned for our Civil Services.

There does not seem much advantage in just taking only bright and intelligent candidates. The candidates must show strength of character, honesty, a desire to help the down trodden, and a capability to rough it out in inhospitable places. They should be passionate about making a difference, standing up in the face of unreasonable demands and not hesitant in giving the right advice. They must be bold and courageous. The right man in the right place can and will tackle loopholes in the system and schemes but the wrong man will look for loopholes even where none exist.

I worked in UP for more than thirty years. It was an extremely frustrating experience but as I was not empanelled, that is, found fit to work in Government of India as Joint Secretary, I had no other option but to continue to work in UP till my retirement. Government of India has a process to select officers fit to come on central deputation to the Government of India. This process is called empanelment and starts from the level of Joint Secretary which means at about sixteen to seventeen years of service in the IAS. A committee goes through ten years' Annual Confidential Reports of all the officers for the post of Joint Secretary. The competition is so stiff that it is said that even if all but one of the reports is not 'outstanding', you may not get empanelled. The empanelment process is also carried out at the level of Additional Secretary and Secretary. As I did not have all outstanding reports, I was not empanelled. Keeping in mind the subjective manner in which these reports are usually given I reconciled to this reality, however unfair, very early in my career.

21

Administration in the UP Secretariat

ADMINISTRATION in the State of UP is fraught with problems. The State has been unable to implement the simplest of orders. The lack of system or administration in UP ironically starts from the headquarters of the UP Government, the very place which is expected to ensure system and administration in the entire State!

The Secretariat comprises several departments. Each department has several sections, of about ten to fifteen clerical staff, which look after particular areas of the work of the department. The officers and the sections of the same department in the UP Secretariat are scattered over various buildings. The Secretaries to the department, their sections and other subordinate officers are seated in offices in different buildings. Even when an officer is transferred from one department to another, he does not vacate his room. He prefers to hold on to it as he may have got the room done up comfortably and often luxuriously, according to his liking, spending the scarce funds of his department. When Shri AP

Singh was Principal Secretary, Sugar Department he had redone his office with a false ceiling and chandeliers making it look like the lobby of a five star hotel. He therefore never shifted out of that office room despite having been posted out of the department. The jobs of the officers change but they continue to sit in the same office room instead of shifting to a room next to their department. Personal convenience is considered far more important than the convenience of the department in ensuring free flow of work. The politicians in UP interfere in the pettiest of things and officers do not hesitate to approach them even for simple things like allotment of office rooms. Over the years this has resulted in a totally chaotic situation. Peons can be seen carrying files from one building to another, stopping for tea on their way. This is utter waste of time and manpower in a system where files have to be carried from one building to another. In this day and age, when e-governance is the norm, the system operating in the State is anachronistic, reprehensible and deplorable.

It is not to say that attempts were not made by the UP Secretariat administration to organize seating of departments in a compact manner. This would be first disrupted by a few officers who chose to break the discipline and then it would soon degenerate into a free-for-all. To get over this chaotic situation attempts were made whenever a new building became functional to locate departments in it with a floor-wise seating plan. But this also degenerated into the chaos that is normally seen in the Secretariat, with the added disadvantage of some officers functioning from buildings with their departmental colleagues or sections functioning from a different building. There was not only lack of self-discipline in the officers themselves, there was also no one to discipline them. The head of administration namely the Chief Secretary thought it was too small a matter for consideration. The head of the Secretariat Administration Department did not have the clout to discipline colleagues. Moreover, they perceived being posted to the Secretariat Administration Department as being 'dumped' or 'punished'. Therefore, they preferred not to get involved in this matter. Their time on the other hand was full managing the unions of the Secretariat employees. Thus, reorganizing or bringing order into the Secretariat seating plan was on nobody's agenda.

The unwieldy government machinery in the Secretariat is lackadaisical about decision making. The same files go back and forth many times. Innumerable reminders are sent asking for information or for reports. The idea is not to ensure that the report or information is received but to keep oneself in the clear. The mindset of officers is such that they are more concerned with avoiding responsibility rather than settling issues. If questions are asked about delay, they are safe because responsibility cannot be fixed on them as they have sent so many reminders. The effort is not directed towards smooth and quick decision making but towards ensuring that one is not faulted. One's table needs to be clean even though there has been no work related contribution.

The file moves through so many levels before any matter can be decided. The lowermost functionary initiates the file. His recommendations go through the Section Officer, Under Secretary, Deputy Secretary, Special Secretary and then to the Secretary and Minister. The file goes up this hierarchy with everybody endorsing the same view. If a senior official wants a different view or recommendation, he will normally call his subordinate and ask him to change his note. He does not have the courage to record his views. Most of the officers are just sending files up and down with no contribution whatsoever. It is very rare that an officer will take a view contrary to the one that has already been recorded. They do not have the courage to overrule their subordinates. One even gets files asking for permission to send a reminder. The file under the circumstances passing through so many levels serves no purpose. It only wastes a lot of time as every stage takes a few days.

Nothing gets done routinely. Every small issue has to be pursued. If pursued doggedly it will take a couple of weeks, if not it may lie untouched for months. Every officer knows that even a leave application has to be pursued so that the order is issued in time. The public is convinced that unless you get a recommendation, your work will not be done. For the simplest of routine work people have to get somebody to speak on their behalf. It is difficult to meet anyone. No one picks up their official mobile phone if the number is not listed and is not important enough. It is a very frustrating experience. I don't see why officers should be given official mobile phones if they are going to use it only for their personal matters. Instead of assuming their role as one of serving the people, government officials think themselves to be the masters of the public. Many officers think themselves no less than 'Maharajas'. It is impossible even for senior officers to get in touch with officers of UP, specially the District Magistrates. They are inaccessible. As soon as they become District Magistrates their demeanour changes. They begin to think that they have inherited a kingdom. It is like they are living in an impregnable fortress.

Delegation of authority is extremely important but non-existent in the UP administration. We find that even inconsequential matters like leave applications of officers require the sanction of the Chief Minister in UP. You can imagine the number of files that the Chief Minister has to see and the time that they will take to clear them. The Chief Minister and the ministers are caught up in routine matters. Files are unnecessarily sent to them. Officers no longer want to take any responsibility for any decision and keep sending every file to the minister. The ministers too want their finger in every pie, and so are quite happy. One of the reasons is also that they lack calibre and foresight. They have no vision for their department. They show no initiative except where money is to be made. They look for short term goals mainly to fill their coffers. They are not concerned about the people or about making any lasting contribution to the society and so they are happy dealing with such routine matters rather than restricting themselves to serious policy issues. As Secretary of the Department of Renewable Sources of Energy, my minister was Shri Bachcha Pathak, a history-sheeter from Allahabad. 'History-sheeter' is an Indian police term for a criminal with a long record of serious crimes. Shri Bachcha Pathak called me once and complained that I was not sending files to him. I informed him that I send only those files to him which required clearance at the minister's level. Files which were within my powers were being cleared by me and I was not required to send these files to him. He did not appreciate this and soon got me transferred. I do however believe that power has to be delegated and then the strictest action must be taken against cases regarding misuse, delay and harassment. Senior officers must to some extent be free to hear complaints and appeals of the public.

Work which is useless and unnecessary must be drastically curtailed. We find that the same issue keeps coming up continuously again and again. Once a decision is taken in a matter it need not be reopened and matters must be decided within a time frame.

Subordinate offices of the departments, which are primarily entrusted with the work of implementing the schemes are not allowed to work. They are used as perk providers supplying air conditioners for the residences, footing restaurant bills or paying for the servants. They should not be reduced to the level of mere hand maidens or back offices of the department. The department must use its own database and must handle matters on its own, rather than send every letter to the subordinate office for seeking information. All basic data is available in the department but the secretariat staff does not want to work and write to the organizations under them for even sending drafts of letters to be sent by the government. Moreover, there are so many reviews and briefings that the officers find little time to go ahead with the task of implementation. More time is spent on these instead of the actual task of implementation of the schemes. This, I find is an extremely serious issue.

The atmosphere in the Secretariat is not business-like and professional. Endless meetings are held but with no results. Meetings last for hours. They just drag on. I remember

Chief Secretaries who were at times totally ignorant of the matter for which the meeting was called so much so that they had to be briefed about the schemes themselves before decisions could be taken. They are so bogged down in routine useless work that they have no time or even the inclination to see the papers before important meetings. Naturally meetings will be nothing but inconclusive. In UP every officer comes to a meeting with several other junior officers, either because he is ignorant or not confident of handling the issue on his own. All this results in substantial waste of time and manpower.

The officers feel that by holding meetings the whole day, they are doing very important work. But it just stops at that with practically no outcome. Minutes of the meeting take more than a month to arrive. The officers create a false sense of importance and effectiveness around themselves by holding these meetings while nothing actually changes on the ground. A number of seminars and conferences are also held in five star hotels. But to my mind these are totally useless, irrelevant and a waste of money. The problem in our country today is basically one of implementation. The officers should be out in the field.

Meetings begin at six or seven in the evening when it is time to go home. Naturally if there is no discipline regarding office timings you cannot expect employees to reach office by nine thirty in the morning. Officials stroll in by eleven, enjoy extended lunch breaks which may last more than an hour and a half. You will not find any officer back from lunch before three thirty or four pm. Many babus do all their personal work during office hours because they have no time otherwise.

Half-hearted efforts made at times to streamline the system yield no results and make a mockery of the efforts.

Endless cups of tea are served in the Secretariat throughout the day. Anybody visiting is also offered a cup of tea. Cups are strewn around in the corridors. Huge wasteful expenditure is incurred on this. The tea is ordered for one person but the entire staff of private secretaries, typists, peons as well as their guests, all drink tea round the clock. Several times the Secretariat Administration Department has tried to curb this unnecessary expenditure but failed.

There are any number of committees which are set-up for no rhyme or reason. The meetings of some of the Standing Committees attached to every ministry are held ever so often that they hamper the normal functioning of the department and put unnecessary financial burden on it. The members expect expensive gifts at every meeting, otherwise they are known to be unhappy and in the habit of passing caustic remarks. To keep them happy one has to ensure that their physical comforts are very well looked after. In summer, these committees tour around in cooler climes causing unnecessary and wasteful expenditure of time and resources. But when there is an austerity drive, the first thing the Finance Minister's axe falls on are the foreign tours of the bureaucrats!

There are serious interdepartmental coordination problems. Every Secretary thinks that he is presiding over an empire and does not want to let go any aspect of his work even though it should logically be clubbed with another department. On the other hand sometimes there is a problem for example with assembly questions which keep on shuttling from one department to another with everybody washing their hands of them saying that it concerns the other department. Departments do not work as a team and this leads to unnecessary delays and obstacles.

There is a Department of Administrative Reforms at the Centre as well as in the States. It is an important department but only used by the government as a parking slot for an officer who has to be punished or sidelined. It is not expected that the Department of Administrative Reforms will do anything and even if someone applies his mind and suggests some course of action it will never be followed, as there is no political or bureaucratic will to bring about reforms and improve the system. Thus we find that there is no scope for administrative reforms in the State although the need is enormous. Consequently these defunct departments have not been able to make any impact.

Under normal circumstances, officers of UP do not like to join the Government of India because they miss the comforts and lavish lifestyle they have in the State. In UP they can come and go from office whenever they please. They enjoy the use of several cars, servants, the servile attitude of staff and so on. They misuse the facilities for their personal use with impunity. All this makes them feel great and consequently ill at ease and out of their depth in Delhi. Due to the presence of a large number of VIPs in Delhi, they feel lost in the crowd and their ego gets totally deflated.

The confusion in the Secretariat is reflected all over the State. It is generally felt that the public in UP is more indisciplined than the rest of the country. You can enter the State from anywhere and immediately you know the difference. The noise pollution, the filth and the chaos overwhelm you. UP is one of the filthiest States in the country. There is always rubble on the roadside. Heaps of stones and mounts of debris of left over and discarded construction material is a common sight. If the central verge gets knocked down by a vehicle it stays in that state for months and even years. Wherever there are garbage cans there is more garbage outside than inside. Open nallahs and drains are everywhere. New office buildings are soon found defaced with red pan spittle. In the Jawahar Bhawan and Indira Bhawan in Lucknow which house several field organizations, one has to navigate through stray dogs, beggars and the stench of urine to take the lift. In spite of having spent large funds trying to clean up the rivers, they are still heavily polluted. Yamuna and Ganga rivers are no wider than drains now. The water is nothing but sewage. They stink and people continue to throw all kinds of filth into the rivers in the name of religion.

The traffic in the State is chaotic. Due to the laxity of implementation in the State, I have noticed that when drivers enter UP, they immediately unfasten their safety belts and begin to jump red lights. On the other hand when they enter Delhi from UP they first fasten their safety belts. This is because they know that Delhi is stricter in implementing and enforcing traffic rules. In UP the constable may just take a nominal amount and let them off in the very rare case of being apprehended. In cases of road accidents they just stand there listening to both sides fighting instead of arriving at some decision and getting the matter resolved. I have seen public transport with one man solely engaged to blow the horn, creating unbearable stress for other commuters. Jay walking is an extremely serious hazard. People have no consideration for others and are an indisciplined lot. It is a common site to see men urinating in public. The non-provision of common washroom facilities is an extremely serious problem particularly for women who perforce have to restrict their intake of water before embarking on a journey. We find stray cattle, dogs and monkeys roaming free, creating a nuisance on the roads in India. Encroachments are a common sight. People extend on the road outside their house, cover the drains and encroach upon the Corporation's land and enclose it as if it is their own. 'Thelas' (vendor carts) selling fruits and vegetables spill over even onto the expressways and at bus stands where there are crowds confounding the situation still further. Law and order is in a serious mess. Rapes, murders, abductions, and dacoities are commonplace. Industries have left due to extortion and harassment. People do not feel safe, with the result that in many places people literally live in cages, their houses being totally enclosed by grills.

These situations must be tackled immediately. The situation at present demonstrates plain lack of governance. Apathy has long set in amongst the people who feel that the State is beyond reclaim and that nothing can be done in UP.

The construction of public toilets is receiving a lot of attention these days but another task that also requires our immediate attention in order to give a semblance of governance is to remove encroachments. The administration must construct markets in earmarked places so that the custom of shopping on roads and streets can stop. This 'tehbazari' creates a lot of traffic jams, inconvenience and is a very serious safety hazard.

The public has to be disciplined and ruthless compliance has to be ensured. To show results the government must immediately divert its attention to enforcing traffic rules. CCTV cameras should be installed at all traffic junctions so that all offenders can be booked. People must be encouraged to dial and complain of citizens not following rules and their complaints should be seen to their logical conclusion. Subways and foot overbridges must be built and their use strictly enforced. Public toilets must be constructed at regular intervals on highways.

22

Rule of Law and Implementation

WE ARE an indisciplined people, and consequently India is an ill governed country. A very large number of citizens have no fear or respect for the rule of law. Their experience over the years has made them believe that everything can be managed with money, power, and connections, and therefore they take full advantage of the rampant corruption.

This situation has resulted primarily due to two reasons. First, there is the tendency to leave loopholes in the rules and regulations and the second reason is an utter disregard for their sanctity. Elasticity in interpretation and implementation of law has become the norm. Selective enforcement has broken down the sanctity of the rule of law. Therefore loopholes in all the Rules and Acts must be plugged. It is these loopholes which keep the avenues for corruption open. Just to give one small example, the Urban Development Authorities in UP (and perhaps elsewhere) have a provision for 'compounding fees' for construction not in conformity with the building bye-laws. The authorities should clearly lay down what can be built and what cannot be built. It is difficult to understand the logic of allowing a grey zone, that is of leaving some construction, which is not allowed under the bye laws but which can be regularized upon the payment of a fine or 'compounding fees' as they are called. While I was posted in the Noida Authority I took up this matter but there was so much of resistance, both from the staff below and the CEO above, that nothing came out of it.

I can say from the my own personal experience of 36 years in the service that more than half the time of a government officer is wasted in finding out ways and means of how to do what cannot and should not be done. They search for loopholes on how to take a particular decision without attracting criticism. People plead with them to find a way out. 'Kuch to rasta hoga' (there must be some way), 'Aap chahenge to ho jayega' (if you want you can do it) is a common refrain. It is very easy to take decisions if one follows the rule of law. But if there are vested interests and one is looking to help someone out for a consideration, it will be more time consuming. For an effective and efficient system, people need to realize and be assured that the rule of law would prevail under all circumstances. The unfortunate reality however is that there are means by which the rule of law can be bypassed and people know that. Offering a bribe or having an officer threatened and pressurized by the more powerful are just some of the ways. It is beyond doubt that once people realize that rules cannot be broken, they will neither waste their time nor that of the officers in trying to circumvent the system. This message unfortunately has not gone through in India.

Implementation of laws in India is also extremely tardy. They are not efficiently and properly enforced and implemented. They merely remain on paper. Neither the citizens take them seriously nor the law enforcing agencies are serious about implementing them. The need of the hour is to not only amend the outdated and anachronistic laws in keeping with the changing times but once laws have been laid down, to ensure they are followed without exception. If laws are broken, the system should be in a position to enforce them and punish the law breakers. This can only be done by taking swift and strong punitive action against the guilty. This alone can serve as an example to others to adhere to the rules and laws of the country. India is a large country and we cannot have a policeman at every corner. The citizens must perforce become disciplined and responsible.

If the system of justice is known to be fair, swift and ruthless it will act as a very strong deterrent. The system should be such that once the law is broken and the culprit has been caught, he will definitely have to face punitive action. The implementation of Law has to be like the law of 'Karma', relentless and just.

I believe that our system of justice cares more for the accused than for the victim. We don't want capital punishment. We believe we can reform a hardened criminal. We make a hue and cry when prisoners make some handicrafts. The Tihar Jail organizes an exhibition of paintings done by the inmates and tremendous hype is created by the press. Recently prominent coverage was given to the fact that a death row convict had won a gold medal in some diploma course. Nobody thinks about the financial, psychological and physical sufferings of the victims. The victim's scars remain for life, whereas the perpetrators of the crime can start a new life with so much more ease.

23

Corruption and Black Money

CORRUPTION is the single largest reason hampering the development of our country. Greed for speedy acquisition of money and a desire to become rich overnight has taken over and reigns supreme. Idealism has disappeared. An honest person is looked upon as a fool to be pitied and sidelined. It is ironic but the wide acceptance of corruption over the years has actually put the honest officer on the defensive. They are a little shame faced when they are categorized constantly as 'rule bound' or 'stickler for rules' and so on. They are put in jobs which are defunct, require no decision making and are more or less irrelevant to the mainstream functioning of the government.

If the system has to improve, very strict action requires to be taken against the corrupt officials and politicians. They have to be made an example of. Only then can the right message go through and improve the situation. Everybody must know that no one can get away with any wrong doing. Officials will have to enforce honesty and integrity upon themselves and also will have to prevent the political leadership from breaking rules. They will have to learn to not bend backwards when a corrupt officer or minister desires certain actions which do not conform to the rules. We have seen that when the political masters want anything done the whole machinery bends double to implement their orders. On the other hand if a person wants a genuine work done but is not in a position or is averse to greasing palms he can wait for months to get his work done.

In UP we have seen unprecedented levels of corruption. Several ministers have been and are history-sheeters. Chief ministers and ministers have become multi-millionaires during their time in power. People openly talk about the percentage that has to be given for tenders to be accepted. Contractors have to give a particular percentage for all works being executed by them. Money counting machines too were rumoured to have been installed in some offices, including that of Yadav Singh, Chief Engineer of Noida to name one, during one particular Chief Minister's tenure. A few officers and ministers who excel in managing these activities control the entire gamut of operations whereas other officers languish in posts without any work at all. There were officers who have at times been given charge of more than a dozen departments. It is difficult to do justice to one department let alone a dozen departments! During Chief Minister Mayawati's time there were only a few officers who were running the entire government. Navneet Sehgal (UP, 1988) and K Fateh Bahadur (UP, 1981) were handling almost all the important departments between them.

I blame the bureaucrats much more than the politicians. I remember, when we joined service, corruption was not as common among the bureaucrats and what existed was of a very petty nature. We used to hear about a district magistrate who on transfer would walk away with the furniture and curtains of the official residence of the district magistrate or about a bitter fight between two DMs, the outgoing and the incoming, over the sharing of the proceeds of the harvest from the land attached to the residence. It may be mentioned here that most of the District Magistrates residences in UP were and are sprawling bungalows with several acres of land attached to the house. This was an additional source of income as it was used for agricultural purposes and gave a tidy profit those days. The expenditure on inputs was nil as the work was given to the Tehsildar and normally not paid for. There were several bitter quarrels at times about who should reap the harvest. Bungalows of Aligarh, Meerut, Allahabad, Banaras and so on were coveted more so even for their agricultural lands. It is a fact that if one expected a service for which there was no financial provision, money had to come from some other source, not strictly legal. Those days winter tours of officers, visits of dignitaries and VIPs involved money for which there was no provision. The tehsildar of the 'Sadar' or the main Tehsil in the district was normally incharge of VIP duty and he had to provide meals and feasts for the visiting officials and dignitaries. I was told that the lower staff contributed this money. They were naturally not contributing from their own meagre salary. They would then collect bribes from the public.

The situation now of course has crossed all limits. Every time a new government came to power in UP, people felt that the situation could not get worse but we have seen that the situation has been getting from bad to worse. There is no limit to the depths of corruption to which politicians and bureaucrats in UP have descended.

The vice like hold of the cancer of corruption is too well-established in all spheres of the government. I doubt if anyone can get any work done in UP without paying money. Corruption including bribes, tax evasions, particularly in real estate where the property is highly under-valued in the market generates black money and a resultant parallel black economy is thriving under everyone's nose.

One of the reasons for tax evasion is also the extremely high income tax rates. Salaried employees have to pay high tax, as all their payments are in cheque and accounted for. Where payments are in cheque, everything is upfront but where there are cash transactions there is very high tax evasion. People do not pay income tax. It is surprising that in a country with a population of more than 120 crores only around 3.3 crores pay tax. This is just 2.77% of our population. Only about 42,800 people have declared taxable income of over ₹ 1 crore annually and just about 4 lakh people have declared incomes more than ₹ 20 lakhs. These people alone account for 63% of the income tax collected from individuals. These figures were given in a reply to a question in Parliament. There seems to be no dearth of money in circulation so obviously the figures do not tell the actual reality. A global financial study released in 2010 put the current value of illicit money outflow from India to be US $ 462 billion. The resultant, rampant black money economy has created a lot of discrepancies. It is difficult for honest officers to afford a meal at a five star restaurant at their personal expense. But when you visit these places you find uncouth, uneducated people dining out with their large families and driving around in swank cars. Honest civil servants are now beginning to think whether it was such a good idea to work hard to get into the Civil Services. They could have started as petty businessmen who seem to have so much more money and a lavish lifestyle. The Services considered elite at one time are not so any more.

To rectify the situation the income tax net has to be spread wide and it should be simple and direct. The government must punish the tax evaders in such a fashion that nobody dares to avoid it. Besides the strongest action against defaulters, there should also be confiscation of ill-gotten assets and property. The tragedy is that the law-enforcers are also law-breakers.

24

Unproductive Departments and Schemes

BESIDES THE suggestions inherent in the preceding chapter I would like to suggest some changes which will curtail the expenditure in the government and make the functioning more efficient. There are a number of unproductive departments and useless schemes in the government which are a financial drag on the exchequer and it would be a much better idea to close them down.

There are many posts where there is no work. In my own case when I was Chairman of the State Administrative Tribunal in Lucknow, I found that in the nearly one and a half years that I was there I would have signed only a couple of papers and that too relating to the staff's leave applications!

These State Administrative Tribunals were set-up to look after the works relating to vigilance cases referred by the government under the UP Disciplinary Proceedings (Administrative Tribunal) Rules 1947 for report and findings thereon, but these tribunals for the last many years have been totally defunct. There are three tribunals in UP, two headed by two of the senior most IAS officers of the cadre and one by a judicial officer. None of these officers has any work. When I took over in October 2009 there were only five cases in the tribunal. In two cases there were stay orders of the High Court dated 4 April 1989 and 15 February 2006 which the State Government had not as yet got vacated. In the other three cases the matters had been referred to the State Government many years back for some clarification and further information but in spite of periodic reminders the State Government had not responded. They did not want to. Of course no new cases had been referred to the tribunals for the last many years.

The office was situated in Jawahar Bhawan where to reach was a difficult task. You had to work your way up through stray dogs and beggars lying in the lobby. There would be a strong stench of urine as you walked to the lift. The building housed many offices and at one time was a landmark in Lucknow. It is now however known more for indiscipline and union politics. As officers had no work, they did not come to office regularly. We would show up in the office once a month and for all practical purposes were leading retired lives. The government was basically using these posts as parking slots which is one of government's many ways for punishing or harassing officers. Similarly officers who were unwell and required to be hospitalized, could ask to be posted there so that they had time to look after their health. The staff posted there strolled in leisurely at about noon time, drank endless cups of tea, gossiped throughout the day and were very active in employee unions. Indiscipline was at its height and nobody was willing to leash them in. A judicial member of the Tribunal was once actually beaten with a shoe, in the office premises just for taking his driver to task for not reporting on time! No action could be taken against the guilty as the union took an aggressive stand and threatened to strike with the result that the government backed down. An officer was asked to do an enquiry into the incident which never saw the light of day. The humiliated officer did not return to office and after several months of leave was adjusted elsewhere. It was really amazing that no action was taken against the guilty! For these activities in the State Administrative Tribunals, the Government of UP was at that time spending ₹ 1.5 crore annually.

Another post that I held for a couple of months was that of the Secretary of the Department of General Administration. This post too had no work. Once a year the department coordinated a meeting between the army and the civilian administration. Another work was to declare holidays and mourning in the case of the death of a VIP. Day to day there was no work. Officers found it very difficult to pass time but again it was a good posting for those who wanted time to do their PhDs or run a business or oversee the construction of their house! I of course was posted there, courtesy Shri Kalyan Singh, the then Chief Minister of UP as a punishment for recommending the closure of Uptron. Similarly the departments of Languages, Religious Affairs, Program Implementation, Sericulture and so on do not even have half day's work and need not be separate departments. A lot of money is being spent on running these departments which are totally unproductive. By looking at these things an enlightened State Government can curtail a lot of unnecessary and wasteful expenditure, instead of routinely issuing inane and routine circulars for reduction in government expenditure.

There are many systems or processes in place for winding up departments which had lost their relevance, either because of change in government policies or because of the creation of other departments. A committee headed by the Chief Secretary was expected to and had identified departments for closure but no further action was taken or could be taken because of the need to have enough number of positions, even if work did not justify them, so that the promotion prospects of officials did not get affected. Some of these positions were also useful for locating officers who wished to be in Lucknow or who had fallen out of favour of the incumbent political dispensation. Over and above, there was probably the feeling among the top most layer of administration that all this was useless work and that there were much better things to occupy oneself with. Even the Finance Department, which would keep worrying about increase in non-productive expenditure and come up with routine and by and large ineffective circulars of reduction in administrative expenditure, would not focus on closing departments. Irrelevant departments and schemes should be wound up immediately and some others with limited relevance can be clubbed with other departments.

Not only are several departments irrelevant there are also several schemes run by the government which are irrelevant. Each department is running so many schemes that it becomes quite a headache and a nuisance to keep track of them. Budget time is quite a task. There are centrally sponsored schemes, there are State sponsored schemes, there are schemes which are given matching grants and so on. The plethora of schemes continue to linger five year plan after five year plan despite having lost their relevance and despite being overtaken by similar schemes. Again, a system is in place for review of all the schemes, merger of schemes and discontinuation of schemes. This exercise becomes extremely relevant when a new five year plan is being formulated but even if this exercise is undertaken, it is more often than not, a formality merely to log that such an exercise has been carried out. The exercise quite often starts very late, leaving very little time for any in-depth understanding and analysis. Often, there are vested interests in terms of incumbent staff, procurement etc. which prevent a decision to abolish a scheme being taken. The exercise does not get the full attention and time of the senior most officials of the relevant departments and the result is that not much comes out of it.

There should be fewer schemes but they must cover all who fall into the category of potential beneficiaries. Once a scheme is decided upon it must be ensured that it covers all beneficiaries and only once the beneficiaries have all been covered and the scheme has outlived its utility, it can be replaced by other schemes. Rather than spread the funds thin over innumerable schemes the money must be spent on a fewer schemes with the intention to cover cent percent beneficiaries. In the absence of such a policy, neither the impact of a scheme is felt nor can the monitoring be done properly.

There is a very serious lack of knowledge among the potential beneficiaries about the schemes available for their benefits. The beneficiaries too are also selected in a haphazard manner. When even educated people like us, in government service, do not know the schemes being offered by some other department how can we expect the poor public to know what is available for them. A maid who had worked for me some years back asked me if there was any scheme for her mother who was old as well as a widow. On checking, I was informed that there is an 'old age pension' scheme, looked after by the District Social Welfare Officer and also a 'widows pension' scheme under the charge of the District Probation Officer. Why can't the same office handle both schemes? Both the officers sat in the District office of Gautam Budh Nagar at Greater Noida. These women were in Noida. I was told that there were several formalities to be completed and a number of forms were required to be filled. The old, uneducated and poor woman would have to travel all the way from Noida to Greater Noida (the existing transport system being very poor), possibly to find that the concerned person is either unavailable in office or on leave. She would waste a whole day. Her daughter too would take leave from her job of doing household chores. I don't know how many trips they would have to make, how much money may be required to be spent on transport and all to get a paltry amount of ₹ 300 a month. So I advised them not to trouble themselves over this pittance. Schemes must not be populist in nature but must justify themselves through the permanent benefits that will accrue to the people. We must remember also that the money being spent is the tax payer's hard earned money and cannot be allowed to be wasted. A total overhaul and a new look at the schemes is urgently required.

In this context I feel that it is imperative that services be provided to the people at their doorstep. This is the only way to ensure that benefits flow to the people. Everybody is aware that people in the villages waste a lot of their time running hither and thither to arrange for seeds, fertilizers, pesticides and other requirements. I feel that there must be a system where basic minimum needs must be supplied to the people at their doorstep. There must be a system whereby a Village Development Officer who should be based in the village itself, could coordinate all the activities in a particular village.

A single window approach is what we talk about for the industry but this single window approach is what is urgently required for the rural village folk. How much time and money is wasted and how much his regular work suffers because he has to go here and there for simple things. With poor infrastructure, poor transport, poor understanding, their simplicity, their diffidence, shortage of money and other related issues, it is not difficult to imagine the trauma a villager faces when he is directed here and there for his work. Very often he has to ask someone else to accompany him, someone else who perhaps has a little more experience and confidence and is a little educated. On top of this he is normally required to give money to make his matter move. Several trips have to be made because sometimes the official concerned is not there, is on leave or has gone for a meeting elsewhere. We find it so difficult to manage all this, let alone an illiterate villager. You can imagine a scenario where an unlettered man has to provide surety bonds, indemnity bonds, get notarization of papers done by a notary, provide

PAN number and so on. The unlettered man does not know what he has to do and he does not know what he is signing. Anybody can take advantage of him. Progress depends on education. To understand anything, to be aware and to take advantage of the schemes of the government the people have to be educated. Since our country was unlettered, the literacy rate at the time of independence being only 12%, we should have simplified our Laws, Acts and arranged for the services to be provided to the citizens at their doorstep. We should have simplified our laws, simplified the language, simplified the procedures, cut off red-tapism and unnecessary visits here and there. It is a tragic situation that an unlettered man faces.

It is in this very context, I feel that all graduates from medical colleges and engineering institutes must spend time in interning in the rural areas. This is the only way that we can provide our rural population, facilities of a high order instead of leaving them at the mercy of quacks. I cannot overemphasize that it is not the people who should go to the government offices but the government officials who must visit the people at their doorstep. If the schemes were fewer, even school children of a certain age could be told about the schemes so that they could inform their illiterate parents.

We have to be proactive in dealing with the problems of the people. The government seems to be unaware of the bitter pain, anguish, frustration and rage that people feel when they have to deal with the government. There must be a time frame for disposal of matters. My gardener told me that his father who had retired from the Delhi Zoo was missing since 2004. The family had lodged an FIR immediately, but even after eight years they had not got their family pension. His mother who is old and uneducated had a tough time managing the affairs of the family. The police did not do anything. The family was thinking of going to the court when the man told me about his problem as they didn't know how to go about it. It took me more than a year of persistent follow up to resolve and settle this issue. On their own the family could not have managed this case. These are the problems we have to take care of. It is the government's responsibility that once an employee has gone missing to review and ensure that his family gets the pension on time, rather than them running from pillar to post not knowing what to do.

The amount of money that the government spends on its employees is not commensurate with the output. The entire focus of the bureaucracy is to push files and not to provide solutions. Every officer is interested that his table remains clean and he is not held guilty and responsible for any delay. For this he will make any query and ask for information which may not really be relevant in deciding the case. More money is spent on maintaining the staff and paying their salary than on the schemes themselves. This is all unproductive expenditure and needs a relook.

The government also unnecessarily exercises controls on which it spends a lot of time, energy and money. I give a few simple examples. The government maintains an army of staff to clear and reimburse the medical bills of the employees. All the checks and balances cannot control misuse and fake bills and I have seen this happen at very high levels too. Moreover, the delays caused by all this checking in reimbursement also creates anger and frustration among the officers. Except for cases of surgery, I think that it would be much better to fix a reasonable amount of money as medical allowance and then leave it to the employees. After retirement too, I find that there is much hassle involved in going to the CGHS dispensary. One has to make a couple of visits every month as it issues medicines only for one month at a time. Every time some medicines are not in stock and one has to wait for their indent and supply. These days, when one can telephone the chemist and get the supply immediately at home, the system prevailing in the government seems rather archaic.

If we look at the leave travel concession scandal that broke out recently we find that officers at the highest level have been misusing this facility and raising very high fake bills. Why should the government spend so much time, energy trying to regulate and control a matter when they can simply fix an amount for LTC and HTC and let the government servants do what they want to do with it. If the government wants to give a facility the best would be to give that facility and forget to control it. When you impose restrictions then you have to monitor that and a lot of manpower, money, time and energy is wasted which serves no useful purpose.

It is also of the utmost importance to ensure that the cost of inefficiency and corruption is not added onto the tariffs and costs of services. I remember that as Special Secretary, Power Department, whenever there was talk about the mounting losses of the UP State Electricity Board, the engineers would always put up a proposal for increasing the power tariff to tackle the situation instead of increasing the efficiency of the Board. That the transmission and distribution losses were as high as 40%, and that they were entitled to free power for the rest of their lives, were matters of no consequence.

Local self-governance has to be strong. If local matters can be handled at the local level it will be beneficial for all. The petty disputes, the litigations which lead to court cases and other issues can be settled with no wastage of time, money and energy. Moreover, a strong and effective local self-government is the only way to reduce the pressure and ease the burden on the government machinery.

In this context, I would like to touch upon the Khap system which has come in for a lot of criticism these days. There is a lot of frenzy about their retrograde ideas. Everybody including the media and social activists are decrying their medieval mindset and deriding their ideas. The Khap system as I remember it from my childhood was quite modern in its outlook but I suppose that here too the degradation seen all around in the country has permeated into the local administration. The sarpanch and the members, once looked up to with respect have now stooped to making money through illegal ways in implementing the schemes.

I am a Jat woman from the Khap-dominated western UP. My husband is a Tamil Brahmin. When I married him in 1979, it was my grandfather in the Khap-dominated western UP village who was my strongest supporter. It was he, who in 1952, sent my father to the USA to do his PhD.

Many times during the summer holidays in our childhood and into our early teens we were sent by my parents to spend several weeks in our ancestral village in order to get to know our roots and be familiar with village life. I and my siblings freely roamed the village, the fields and the outskirts exploring our surroundings and enjoying ourselves. Even in our early teens my sister and I were never asked not to venture alone by my grandparents. In fact they would often send us on errands to the fields which could be some distance. I don't recall any untoward incident or any sense of fear or insecurity in spite of the potentially dangerous environment which existed at the time in the rural areas, as I realize now.

Only a few well to do households in the village had toilets. Everybody else had to go out into the open. Even young girls and women had to go out into the fields. Moreover there was no electricity in the villages those days and life would come to a standstill soon after dark. The only source of light was a kerosene lantern and its use was kept to the minimum. The fields were scattered as Chakbandi or consolidation proceedings had not as yet been completed. Women used to be equally active in the house and outside, either working or supervising or doing innumerable errands which are a part and parcel of farm life. Also people in the villages do not live in isolation unlike in the cities. They are in and out of each other's houses. In this potentially dangerous and unsafe environment women moved around freely.

The reason for this widespread sense of security and freedom in the villages was due to the Khap or the Panchayat administration. It is the Khaps who have over the years ensured by and large a civilized society in the villages where the girls could roam freely without fear of attack, unlike today. The ban against the same Gotra and same village marriages was only to ensure that no liaisons could develop in the village, so that girls were safe from sexual exploitation. So when every man in the same village was conditioned to look upon the women in the village as his sisters, women had not much to fear. The Khaps have also done yeoman service as far as dowry and widow remarriage were concerned. Demands for dowry and widow harassment were unheard of in our community.

The success of the system was also due to the fact that the tolerance level for any deviation was zero, irrespective of connection, standing etc. The punishment that was meted out to anybody who deviated from the right path was ostracization which in local parlance was 'Hookah Pani Bandh', a punishment worse than death or in extreme cases the person was banished from the village and was never to show his face in the village again. Under these strict codes, crime against women was rare.

To keep the population on the right path, they must be assured of justice and fair play in every field. And if perchance someone has to take recourse to the judiciary for redressal, justice must be inexpensive and quick. When I was placed under suspension by Ms Mayawati, I had thought of going to court but the kind of expenditure involved both with regard to lawyers' fees and other miscellaneous expenditure, put me off. Miscellaneous expenditure included expenditure on translating every paper in Hindi to English, getting every letter retyped on a special kind of paper, of a particular size and in a special kind of font. What is all this if not harassment? Justice has to be inexpensive and quick.

Another reason for the increasing number of frivolous cases in my opinion is that the administrators, particularly the policeman are not doing their work. They behave like bystanders. They take no action even if people approach them. Many crimes could have been avoided, had the police taken action on the complaints of the victims. They let situations fester and foment thinking that the problem will take care of itself and intervene only when the damage has already been done. Due to this attitude of the police, the people have lost all respect for the force. The law-breakers are so bold and fearless of the police that if you threaten them that you would report them to the police, they would taunt you by saying "jail bhijwa do" (get us sent to jail). The police force is insensitive and incommunicado even with people like us so their attitude towards the poor public can be well imagined. These are matters of the gravest concern.

25

Education and Character Building

EDUCATION and character building are of the topmost priority in India today. These two together I feel can take care of most of the ills that we face today. Education is a very vast subject and there are any number of problems which everybody is aware of. But the issues I would like to stress on are uniformity in syllabus and knowledge of English.

India is a vast country with several languages and several examination boards. A lot of rural students and particularly those who are studying in the regional medium are at a disadvantage when they have to compete and move to urban areas. So I feel that it is also necessary that the medium of instruction should be in English throughout the country so that all are on a level playing field. I have seen innumerable people not making it big and exploiting their full potential because of their lack of command over the English language. In today's times in India knowing English is more important than anything else to move up the ladder. If you don't speak English people look down upon you. This is a fact which we have to recognize and accept. Our rural population is at a great disadvantage due to the poor quality of education and lack of knowledge of English. If we want our rural population to rise and compete on an equal footing with the urban elite and have the right exposure we must provide them with good educational facilities and improve their command over the English language. This 'Great Divide' as I call it has to be tackled. The mindset of people with knowledge of English is different. It gives them a lot of exposure. There is a huge difference between the urbane English speaking class and the mostly rural class which has been educated in the vernacular. The country has to move together. Although our own languages are very important, fluency in English is essential in today's world. You cannot deny the exposure that knowledge of this language gives. India is a diverse country with diverse languages, people have to converse with people of other States. Officers in service have to speak with foreign delegations and therefore keeping all these things in mind we have to encourage knowledge of English.

I feel that in India we should also think about having a uniform examination board and a common syllabus in all schools. One of the main problems that people face when they are transferred from one place to another is the tough task of getting their children adjusted to new boards, new syllabuses and so on. Ensuring continuity of education with the same Board is a major problem and so if people know that proper schools are available everywhere and their children will not be disadvantaged they will not resist their transfers. This will also save them extra expenditure of maintaining two households.

Character building is the most important task in front of the country today and only education can build it. All innovations, schemes and reforms will fail unless we improve the character of our citizens. The education system besides giving the children knowledge of various disciplines and subjects, has also to make them good human beings. All the right attitudes and right values have to be inculcated in schools. Most of the ills in the society that we are facing today can be tackled only by our education system. To take the country forward education is the one thing we have to concentrate on and rest of the things will follow. It will make the task of everyone else so much easier. Crimes will come down. Corruption will be leashed in. The money will reach where it should but unfortunately it is character and good values that we are lacking today that is responsible for our ills.

We keep hearing the word 'Aam Admi' but who is the Aam Admi? The Aam Admi is the supposedly less affluent person with not much influence or power. It is a person who cannot hope to get any undue consideration over and above the system that normally prevails everywhere. But is the Aam Admi as much a victim as he is made out to be or is the Aam Admi frustrated and angry because he does not command extra attention and he is envious of others who do? Will the Aam Admi remain the Aam Admi if he has money, power and influence. Will he then think of the person who does not? Will his heart then cry for the Aam Admi?

I feel that there is nobody or no such character as an Aam Admi in India. The Aam Admi cries because he does not have the opportunity to take advantage. If he gets an opportunity he too will do the same. The rickshaw puller, taxi drivers, vegetable vendors, shopkeepers and petty government officials. Are these not characterized as Aam Admi? They are but when they get an opportunity they also exploit the others to the best of their ability. It is the Aam Admi in India who lacks character and it is that which is responsible for the problem we face today. If the Aam Admi had integrity, if the Aam Admi stood adamant on the right path, if the Aam Admi taught his children the right values then we would not be in the position we find ourselves in today. If the Aam Admi can get swayed at the time of elections by a bottle of liquor, by a dhoti, by a pressure cooker then what is the character of the Aam Admi? We talk proudly of being the largest democracy but if this is the situation then what democracy are we talking about? The Aam Admi must be the backbone of the country. But India has also been failed by its Aam Admi. If the Aam Admi had maintained his character, he could have prevented the system from failing in this fashion.

26

Civil Services

CIVIL SERVICES play an extremely important role in the growth and development of the country. They are the torch bearers of the system. As George Bernard Shaw said, "Life is no brief candle to me. It is a sort of splendid torch that I have got to hold up for the moment and I want to make it burn as brightly as possible before handing it on to future generations." This is exactly the role that the civil servants must look to perform. The human element is the most important factor in the success of any programme. If the intentions of the persons incharge of implementation are good, the advantages will flow to the people even if the schemes are not so good. In the process of implementing a scheme a good officer will ensure its success at his own level. Unfortunately the civil servants today do not enjoy a good reputation for integrity. They were to act as the pillars of the system but unfortunately except for a handful the pillars have collapsed under the weight of their political masters and their own greed!

In the changed scenario I feel that several changes in the system of recruitment and assessment of the calibre of the civil servants is a must. The civil servants are recruited by a system which lays the maximum emphasis on a written examination. But what we need in service today is character. Examinations are fine but examinations cannot judge the character of a person. I feel that the person's character and personality are of the utmost importance in the service. If a person lacks character and is unable to withstand pressure, is greedy, is lazy, then he is of no use even if he is intelligent. A public servant must have the highest values and an impeccable character. There must be some way to judge the character of the candidates who appear for the Civil Services Examination. A person's sense of right and wrong, his ability to stick to his principles against all odds, his ability to withstand pressure, his desire to help the down trodden, these are the traits that one must look for in public servants.

I was recently invited by the UPSC to be a member on the interview board for recruiting Civil Services aspirants. The qualities that the candidates were to be assessed for included social traits, mental alertness, critical power of assimilation, clear and logical exposition, balance of judgement, variety and depth of interest, ability for social cohesion and leadership as well as intellectual and moral integrity. Although the half hour, determined for the interview did give one some inkling of the candidates overall capabilities, his power of expression, the width of his knowledge and the strength of his personae, it was difficult to gauge his character. They come prepared to give politically correct answers. I felt that to do justice to the selection process perhaps we should have a test where we can observe them, say over a week and then select them. Although all candidates are on probation for a two year period, this provision has rarely been invoked. Even extending the probationary period is very rare. We, Indians can never take a decision to terminate a candidate's career even if he deserves it, due to our misplaced sense of not causing harm to anyone.

I feel that in the Indian Foreign Service the personality and the conduct of the candidate is even more important than in the IAS. His power to impress others should be stressed upon. On my travels abroad I have had occasion to meet new entrants into the Foreign Service. I am sorry to say that at times one feels ashamed to see these officers who are representing our country abroad. The way they conduct themselves, their ability to express themselves, and their demeanour are far from impressive. I feel that the earlier policy when minimum marks in the interview were a must for Foreign Service recruits, was right. The main task of the Foreign Service officers is to project our country abroad. The personality counts for a lot in this service.

I feel that it is not in keeping with the recruitment of the best talent if we keep on increasing the age of the candidates who take the exam and let them have unlimited chances to sit for it. Earlier on too the Scheduled Caste and Scheduled Tribe candidates were being recruited in the service, so the necessity of downgrading the system by increasing the age limits and number of times a candidate can sit for the examination is unclear. The age limit of the General category candidates is now 32 years and they can make up to six attempts, that of the OBC candidates is 35 years and they can make up to seven attempts and that of the Scheduled Caste candidates has been increased to 37 years and they can have recourse to unlimited number of attempts. It is a little surprising why at this stage after so many years, instead of increasing the standard we are downgrading the qualifications. This also clearly shows in the kind of candidates being selected now. I think we should be worldly wise, look to the future and improve the standard of the candidates selected. I personally feel that the candidate should not be given more than three attempts. If he is good, he should come through the second attempt only. If not, he is not up to the mark.

The system of assessing the performance of the officers in service is also fraught with shortcomings. Professionalism is totally lacking. Officers who are sycophants and can keep the boss happy by agreeing to whatever he says even if it is wrong are the ones who very often are able to secure outstanding performance reports and go up high in the hierarchy. Human nature being what it is, bosses prefer if the juniors boost their ego and behave like doormats. Subordinates who are on very good terms with their bosses for whatever reason, are even asked to write their own performance reports and just get it signed by the boss. I know of so many officers who are incapable but because of their acquiescent nature and the ability to keep their bosses happy have outstanding reports. Officers with an independent mind find it very difficult. Although the writing of a confidential report will always have a strong element of subjectivity, we must try to minimize it.

I was not empanelled as Joint Secretary because of the bad experiences I had with my seniors from an early time and the less than outstanding reports I received from them. I of course learnt very early to curtail my ambition and to take a conscious decision that for my own peace of mind I should forget about Annual Confidential Reports. This relieved me to a great extent from any tension regarding my boss. In a working environment it does not take long for relationships to sour. There are bound to be disagreements. Things may be working out smoothly and suddenly there maybe a disagreement over an issue and the relationship comes under a strain, putting an end to one's hopes of earning an outstanding entry. Even in an official setting, disagreements are taken personally.

The problem is that officers lack courage of conviction and are therefore hesitant to take responsibility. If they know that they are right then there should be no hesitation in overruling their subordinates and taking responsibility for their decision but now they do not want to be in a position where they will have to overrule and disagree with a subordinate in writing. They feel that if the matter comes up later, they can always say that the recommendation had come from the office, they had only agreed with it and that the responsibility is solely that of the proposer.

A person's character does not remain a secret for very long. Everybody in service knows about everybody else. The activities a person indulges in, very soon become common knowledge. A person may have outstanding written reports but his spoken reputation may be bad. On the other hand a person may enjoy a very good reputation for effectiveness, integrity and hard work but his Annual Confidential Reports may be just about average. The system must take cognizance of an officer's spoken reputation also. I strongly feel that the senior's assessment too must also be done by his juniors to get a correct picture from the other side. I have very often found that good subordinates are more often than not bad bosses. They ingratiate themselves with their superiors and expect juniors to behave in the same fashion.

Hardly ever is any action taken in UP against an officer for wrong doings. Enquiries are set-up and they continue indefinitely. Vigilance cases go on for years. We never heard of any case where strict action was taken against an officer. In UP particularly there were several officers whose notorious reputation everybody in the State knew but against whom the State Government took no action. As the government did not take action, the UP IAS Officers Association embarked on the novel scheme of voting the three most corrupt officers of UP. Two of these Shri AP Singh of the 1967 batch and Smt Neera Yadav of the 1971 batch went on to become Chief Secretaries of the State in spite of being embroiled in controversies and enquiries. Much later when public interest litigations were filed against them did the court take action and both had to spend some time behind bars. On the other hand you find that action is taken against an unpliable officer on some trumped up charge. I was placed under suspension on a non-issue namely that I had not waited for the sanction letter of the State Government before proceeding on a two day private visit to Sri Lanka on casual leave. The real reason of course was that I had not agreed to the irresponsible and illegal master plan of the Yamuna Expressway Authority. On the other hand, to give just one example, Shri Pradeep Shukla of the 1981 batch who was involved in the National Rural Health Mission scam (which also saw the murders of three Chief Medical Officers) and who spent a couple of months in jail before being let out on bail was initially not even placed under suspension but was posted as Member in the Board of Revenue, the apex body for revenue administration, while out on bail!

I also feel that there are some jobs in the government which require some specialization. Although the experience of IAS officers is such that they may not take too much time to familiarize themselves with the functioning of a new department. I still feel that there are certain jobs which do require technical expertise. Moreover, the government's role as I see it is to regulate and monitor and not get into direct commercial operations.

The general feeling in the bureaucracy is that the system is not fair and that merit is not recognized. Individual connections play a dominant role. Favouritism and nepotism flourish. Money power has also now become crucial and many officers were known to buy their so-called lucrative jobs in UP. It is a well-known fact that lucrative jobs required money to be given. Caste and regional equations also matter a great deal. When Ms Mayawati comes to power, the Scheduled Caste officers have the upper hand. They occupy most of the so-called important jobs. Her secretariat too will be occupied by officers of the Scheduled Castes. When Shri Mulayam Singh comes to power, Yadavs are omnipresent.

Officers also form strong networks based on their castes. In UP the Kayastha lobby, the Brahmin lobby, the Baniya lobby and the Scheduled Caste lobby have traditionally been very strong. Many officers who are doing well are doing well for considerations other than merit. They could be either total doormats and yes-men or they are well-connected. If officers feel that the system has not been fair to them, they will be left with a brooding sense of injustice and are not going to give off their best.

The political environment has thoroughly deteriorated. Earlier there were some norms and the politicians seemed to know their limits. Protocol was followed. Working on minister's verbal orders was unheard of and all orders were sent to the departments in writing. Now of course this is not the case. Now, ministers are even known to have said in meetings that even if a particular person, who is close to them, says something then it should be given the same importance as if these were the minister's orders.

Many of the ministers and politicians in UP are history-sheeters with a long list of criminal charges against them. There are any number of ministers who are charged with heinous crimes like murder, dacoity and drug smuggling. They are in politics for the express purpose of amassing wealth and not for nationalism and public service. Politics is considered very good business and has now become a family business which is inherited by a person's heirs. Over the years we have seen that nothing happens to these politicians and they go scot-free. This sends a strong message that if you are powerful then you can get away with anything. They moreover accept only pliable officers who will do their bidding and facilitate their interests. In fact, it is impossible not to get a posting in any department unless the minister so desires.

The spectre of frequent transfers and the consequent disturbance hangs like a Damocles' sword over the heads of the officers. Frequent transfers particularly those which require a change of place create a lot of disturbance. You may not get a residence in a new place for several months and will have to put up in guest houses. Children's education will get disrupted and smaller places may not even have good schools. You may get posted to a place where there may be no facilities whatsoever and consequently the feelings of humiliation and loss of face are also problems which require to be tackled. There are officers who have had to face transfers as frequently as twice or thrice a month. The politicians are using this weapon of frequent transfers to their advantage. The Appointments Department of the UP Government has now totally lost its relevance. It has become a mere post office for issuing the orders. The decisions are taken elsewhere and they are only intimated to the Appointments Department for issuing the orders. It is the minister's prerogative to decide on who he wants as his Secretary. There is hardly anything that happens on merit. Under these circumstances the officers find themselves in the unenviable position where they either toe the line of the minister or face frequent transfers and subsequent problems. Some of the officers who are honest may unfortunately be lacking in courage and acquiesce. They try their best to escape responsibility but at the same time are not capable of taking a stand because otherwise they will find themselves in the unsavoury position of having to face frequent transfers, no posting, forced leave and harassment of this kind which they are either unwilling or unable to handle.

As there is no stable tenure, the officers just mark time pushing files as and when they come rather than taking initiative to improve the system. If an officer knows that he will be in a particular job for some length of time, he will pay more attention to the job and see things in the perspective of long term goals. Many officers go through their careers just learning. As soon as they come to grips with the work, they find themselves on another job.

The whole scenario has had a very deleterious effect. Subordinates have lost faith in their senior officers. Everybody knows that if they take a stand, which may go against the political will, their senior officers too will not support them. Officers in trouble find no support from any quarter. Nobody is going to stick his neck out for anybody. There are instances where if a particular officer is not in the good books of the political masters then, other officers too will shun him. A police officer in UP who got on the wrong side of the government for pointing out some irregularities in the recruitment of constables was even declared mentally unfit. Team spirit, brotherhood, standing by one another are sentiments of a by gone era. Now everybody is on his own and individual interests are of paramount importance. In the last thirty years I have seen the bureaucracy steadily deteriorating before my eyes.

Motivation in the Civil Service, particularly in UP is non-existent. Nepotism and favouritism flourish. Officers with ministers get good postings of their choice. Post retirement jobs go to officers close to ministers and so on. Such activities motivate no one. In fact I am of the firm opinion that the government must do away entirely with post retirement jobs. There are any number of avenues open for self-engagement outside the government and these retired officers must make way for the junior officers.

27

Training

I HAVE FOUND that the calibre of a large number of government employees is very low. The department comes to depend on a few key persons who are competent. Instead of wasting time on the ones who are not, we keep loading the competent ones. Something is definitely wrong with our recruitment system. Recruitment must be strictly on the basis of merit and once recruited the training of the employees has to be taken up very seriously.

Utter lack of training can be seen in the way traffic constables can be seen on duty in UP. They hardly look like the State's police force, so casual and laid back in their approach. In UP you will see them with their back towards the traffic, eating pan or sitting on the mobike and gossiping on their mobile phones while the traffic is totally chaotic. Once on my way, I saw three private buses racing one another. First one would overtake then the other and so on, honking continuously. I rang up the Police Helpline No 100 about what was happening with the request that they should intercept them and book them for rash driving. But it was such an obtuse man at the other end who insisted on wasting time asking for my full name, address and what not, even though I told him that I was a retired government officer. I had to tell him that there was no time to waste and he must get on with the job or there might be some serious mishap. He had the gumption to tell me that if I didn't give him all my particulars he will not do 'my work'. I told him that it was not 'my' work but that I was trying to help the police to do their work. These are the kind of people we have to deal with who have no understanding, no initiative and no sense of responsibility. Their attitude is that they are doing you a favour. When I complained about this attitude to the District Magistrate she could only giggle!

There is a plethora of staff with no understanding whatsoever and without an open mind. Sometimes it is impossible to get across. It is therefore extremely important that proper training and proper assessment of the capabilities of the employees must be done. The probationary period is precisely for this reason. If it is felt that an individual is not up to the mark then obviously he must not be confirmed in service. However, I presume that this cannot be done when employees of this level buy their jobs and enter the service after paying large sums of money. In UP we heard that the going rate for the recruitment of constables was pegged at ₹5 lakh. So if money is what gets you the job then you will only work towards earning money in your service career. Candidates too are paying to enter government service because they know that they will not only recover the amount paid but will make much more money. There is rampant corruption in recruitment. When candidates enter by giving hefty amounts of money, they can have no other ambition except to make money. So one really cannot expect any work from them.

28

VIP Culture

FEW COUNTRIES have the VIP or the Very Important Person culture that we have in India. The citizens of India are not equal. There are either ordinary citizens or the VIPs.

There are various ways in which to distinguish an ordinary citizen from a VIP. A red or blue beacon on the vehicle is the first sign of a VIP. Then their vehicle will also have 'Government of India', 'Bharat Sarkar' or a particular 'State Government' name inscribed on it. Particularly in UP, government vehicles carry big plates in red with the designation of the officer ferried in it inscribed very prominently in brass. This mindset has become so widespread that you find even the village 'Sarpanch' carrying his designation on his personal car. You will also find 'Judge', 'Press', 'Ex-SDM' or whatever else inscribed on private vehicles. The necessity for resorting to these activities indicates and reinforces the belief of the people that if you are not somebody in the government then you will not get the attention you desire. This also goes to confirm that an ordinary citizen in India does not get due attention.

The trappings of power are extremely important in our country. There are certain facilities allowed only to a few designated officials, but you find that all and sundry use these trappings with total impunity. There have been at times some feeble attempts to rectify the state of affairs but when the will is not there, these end up in lack lustre farces which send a very wrong signal to the people. The people must know that if the administration is implementing a policy it has to be ensured that they follow it, not feel that they can mark time and then carry on again as usual.

The bureaucrats and the ministers too must know what life is like for the ordinary citizens in the country. They must be made to face all the problems that a common man faces. They should not be allowed to blare a siren and be escorted through the traffic. Only designated people working for law and order, traffic control, ambulances and firefighting vehicles should be allowed a siren. They must realize that they are the servants of the public and not their masters. You find large contingents of police on the roads when a VIP is going to pass through but never see them otherwise. So except for a few designated vehicles, all these trappings of power in public must be stopped. Only when the bureaucrats, judges and politicians in power face the travails of the common citizens, they will hopefully work for a better service delivery system.

People in important positions appropriate for themselves perks which they should not. Why should ex-Presidents and ex-Prime Ministers be given huge bungalows after they demit office? You enjoy the facilities and perks of holding a post as long as you hold that particular office, but after you demit the post, you should learn to live like an ordinary citizen. We have borrowed our systems from the British but the British Prime Ministers move away from 10 Downing Street immediately on demitting office and drive out of the PM's earmarked bungalow to their private residences, in their own private vehicle. Why is it that we in India spend huge amounts of the taxpayer's money in renovating palatial houses for our ex-Presidents and Prime Ministers?

In UP the practice is that an ex-Chief Minister gets a house for life and very often their heirs continue forever. This has resulted in Chief Ministers earmarking huge properties for themselves and getting them renovated and refurbished for their personal use as soon as they become Chief Ministers. Looking for a suitable accommodation for their post Chief Ministership period is their first task. Large amount of public funds are spent on doing up their houses. Ms Mayawati got the Cane Commissioner's office on Mall Road vacated overnight to build a huge palace for herself. Shri Mulayam Singh Yadav also has appropriated several houses on Vikramaditya Marg for his use. What is the rationale behind these comforts? What service have these people done for the State and the country? What are the sacrifices that they have made? The State of UP has continuously and steadily gone downhill over the years under the misrule of various Chief Ministers.

There is a clamour to have a sprawling Memorial whenever a leader dies. The entire area along the length of the Yamuna has been taken away by various memorials. Their official houses are also converted into museums and national memorials. We have several sprawling buildings and government properties which have been blocked from future use. Government property I feel should not be allowed to be converted into a memorial. We cannot block such properties from being put to more productive work.

Political parties also vie with one another to get the birthdays and death anniversaries of their leaders declared as national holidays. We in India have too many holidays which we must curtail. We can fix the number of holidays a person can take and he can take them depending on what is important for him.

We must stop living in the past. Even after 68 years of becoming an independent country we are still celebrating Independence Day. The British rule has made a very deep impression on the Indian psyche. We have still not got over it. It has been very deeply ingrained. We should celebrate our Independence Day as our National Day. I don't see any reason why we should celebrate a so-called Independence Day and remind ourselves over and over again that we were a slave nation once. Independence is history to be read and taught in schools, not to remind ourselves every year as long as we live.

29

Reservation and Pseudo-Secularism

A FEW very serious issues which also effect governance and administration are our policies of Reservation and Pseudo-Secularism. Whenever there is a compromise, we are playing with governance. Reservation, pseudo secularism and the like fall in this category.

The Constitution of India provided for reservation for the Scheduled Castes and Scheduled Tribes for 10 years after independence. But reservation has continued unabated for nearly 70 years now. To begin with, reservation was there only for the Scheduled Castes and Scheduled Tribes but reservation for the Other Backward Classes (OBC) was also included later. There was a time when people were ashamed to be known as backward. Now all and sundry want to be declared as backwards. Sometimes the Gujjars are agitating to be categorized as backwards, sometimes the Jats are sitting on dharna and creating havoc. The sense of shame in being called a Scheduled Caste or a backward is now over, due to the misuse of reservation. Bright and meritorious students fail to get admission in medical and engineering colleges and in jobs which go to the reserved category who may be much below them in the merit list.

I think we have been thoroughly irresponsible in the task of ensuring the development of the country, in our greed to be in power at whatever cost. This policy of reservation has had severe reactions. On the one hand the differences between the people have widened. Caste divisions today are worse. The forward castes who were feeling ashamed of their misdeeds in the past and were keen to make amends, have been alienated due to the policy of reservation and the aggressiveness of the Scheduled Castes. The caste divide has deepened. The undue advantages of reservation by the creamy layer is also adding oil to the fire. Children of many of the Scheduled Caste IAS officers prepare for the Civil Services and qualify due to reservation. There are several Scheduled Caste officers in UP whose children are also in the IAS. The education and upbringing of these children has not been any different from children whose parents belong to the so-called higher castes. We see many children of these people getting into the Civil Services, IIMs and IITs solely on the basis of the reservation policy.

Having had a very cosmopolitan upbringing and having been educated in metro cities of Delhi, Mumbai and Chennai, I became aware of the seriousness of the caste issue only when Shri Baburam, Commissioner (Jhansi) ruined his relationship with me over the suspension of a Block Development Officer who happened to belong to the Scheduled Caste. His caste loyalty to a fellow Scheduled

Caste whom he had perhaps not even seen was much more than to his junior colleague in the service who was suggesting a course of action solely on the basis of that person's performance. Children, today of course are now aware about the caste system at a much younger age.

Caste politics has thoroughly divided the country. Everybody knows that elections are fought on basis of caste. The candidates are selected based on caste equations in a particular constituency. Extensive research is done on the demographic constitution in the constituency before giving a ticket to a candidate. All political parties mouth inanities about no distinction between caste and religion but this can never come to pass unless we scrap the policy of reservation. No political party or any member of a political party today has the courage to raise this demand of doing away with reservation and announce that for all policy decisions the only difference we should acknowledge is that of the privileged and the under privileged. In fact today you will find that several Scheduled Caste families are better off than the families belonging to forward caste.

It is also a fact that reservation promotes complacency amongst the beneficiaries who may not strive hard to improve their lot. In UP at one time the government had ordered that Scheduled Caste candidates will be entitled to seats in medical colleges even if they get zero marks! A person not of a certain calibre will drag the system down. Standards of service are therefore hit and this promotes a culture of mediocrity. Efficiency and capability must be the sole criteria for selection. We cannot have teachers, doctors, engineers who have not been selected on the basis of merit.

Ms Mayawati had begun to enforce reservation in promotions also. What can be more demotivating and devastating than to begin working under a person who till recently was working under you?

A policy that was envisioned by the framers of the Constitution for just ten years now seems to be overtaking all spheres of life. There does not appear to be an end. It is high time reservation on the basis of caste is scrapped and political parties look at more innovative and substantive issues of policy making to garner votes. I don't think anybody would have any quarrel with an underprivileged person getting all facilities like free education, special coaching institutes, free books etc. but in the end only hard work and merit has to be rewarded. Merit is the only criteria on which recruitments and selections can be made. There can be no other, if we want our country to progress.

Another important issue which perhaps we have failed to look at is that if we do away with the reservation, then the Scheduled Castes and Scheduled Tribes will also raise their self-respect in their own eyes as well as in those of others. You cannot get respect and admiration unless you achieve something by dint of your own efforts and merit. Otherwise people look down upon you as having got in by belonging to the reserved category. There was at one time a scheme in UP whereby people marrying Scheduled Castes were monetarily rewarded. I think that this was very insulting. This is not the way to remove caste differences.

The Scheduled Castes must take lead in the matter and ensure that politicians talk about economic policies rather than divide the people on the basis of caste and religion.

Enlightened leaders belonging to the Scheduled Caste today would be doing the greatest service to the country if they declare that the policy of reservation should not continue any longer. Only then can we hope that political parties will be forced to think of issues other than this.

Another issue that has been discussed on and off is the reservation for women in Parliament. I am personally against reservation of any kind. Women in our country have made much headway in the last many years in all spheres of life. They have been able to hold their own without reservation so far. If reservation was required, maybe it was only at the time when we had just become independent. I think at this stage we don't need to take a retrograde step. Women will come up more and more on their own strength as the mindset of people changes with proper education.

Secularism too means that the State would not take cognizance of any person on the basis of religion and that there would be the same rules which would apply to all irrespective of their caste, creed and religion.

On the other hand the entire effort of the country, to show that India is a secular country, has become a joke. The Chief Minister's office in UP will always have a Muslim officer as one of his Secretaries. The Prime Minister's office will always have one officer who is a Muslim. One of the two either the President or Vice-President should be a Muslim. If we are truly secular then we don't have to wear secularism on our sleeve. The rules in a secular country should be the same for everybody irrespective of their religion. There should not be postings because you need a person of a particular religion. Officers cannot be posted to a particular job because one needs a person there belonging to a particular religion.

Religion should be a private matter and no distinction or special facilities should be given to anybody on the basis of their religion. There should be no talk of religion. Both Hindu and Muslim leadership must adopt an enlightened stand.

30

Patriotism

PATRIOTISM in the country is lacking. At one time the National Anthem was played in theatre halls at the end of the movie but you found very few citizens having the patience and the patriotism to stand through. We see real patriotic fervour once in a while, particularly when we have a cricket match against Pakistan. It is not that the people are lacking in patriotism. It is that the spirit is lying dormant. We have not been able to tap this spirit of patriotism which we must if we want to harness our people for the swifter development of our country. One of the reasons for this is that there has been no effective leadership in the country for some time. A leader has to lead by example. You have to be of impeccable character and then only you can also expect the same from others.

The destruction of public and private property by protesters and agitators requires to be tackled very seriously. Whenever there is a protest, agitators begin to damage public and private property. Cars are smashed, trains are burnt and buses destroyed. This damage to the public property cannot be allowed and the strictest action must be taken against the perpetrators of these crimes. These anti social elements must be booked and severely punished. They take advantage of the presence of mobs and the frayed tempers. Once when travelling through UP in the new modern Shatabdi with wide glass windows, some village children on the way threw bricks at the moving train and cracked the glass panes just for the fun of it. Ours is a poor country and we cannot afford to have public property desecrated and defaced like this. All this stems from a lack of patriotism. We don't have a sense of pride in ourselves and our country. Otherwise we would not indulge in such activities.

India is a diverse country rich in heritage. Our diversity, our architectural wonders, our ancient temples, our crafts, our traditions and rituals are unique. Vedas, medicinal system of Ayurveda and Yoga are India's gift to the world. However we have not been able to publicize these to the requisite level and have not been able to capitalize on soft diplomacy. Our old songs and music, our Bollywood movies are very popular in many other countries but we have not been able to influence people and win friends. This is all because we don't take pride in our culture. We still have a slave mentality. Our children are still doing PT or Physical Training instead of learning Yoga and breathing exercises. Unless we take pride in our culture nobody else will.

31

Epilogue

I HAD finished writing my book and was getting in touch with the publishers when the BJP government was voted to power at the Centre and formed the government under the dynamic leadership of Shri Narendra Modi. The new government has taken some steps towards some of the goals that I, and I am sure many others have been thinking about. This has brought hope that perhaps Mr Modi will turn India around and make it a superpower.

I feel that Mr Modi has started the right way. The first and foremost step that anybody would take when they take over a new job or a new house is to clean up the mess and Mr Modi has done just that by starting the 'Swacch Bharat' campaign. India is by far the filthiest country in the world. Even one of the UPA's ministers was quoted as saying that India could get the Nobel Prize for filth. When you ask foreigners what is it that strikes them when they land in India for the first time, they invariably mention besides the colour, the noise and the filth. It is a traumatic experience in India even for us to go to some markets. People spit everywhere. It is an effort to manoeuvre oneself from stepping onto this muck on the road and invariably one has to take a bath on returning home. People do not have toilets and defecate in the open. And this is one sight which can easily be seen at dawn and dusk, especially from a train window. The stench and the mounds of filth on the tracks and on the platforms is one reason why I personally avoid travelling by train although it is so much cheaper. When people return to India after their travels abroad, I am sure that they feel depressed when they compare the standards of cleanliness and aesthetics abroad and the dirt that they see all around them in their own country. Perhaps our standards of hygiene and cleanliness are very low. You do find people eating and drinking from a thela with an open drain and garbage next to it. During the Commonwealth Games, the issue of cleanliness had been much highlighted by the media and we had cut a very sorry figure. In spite of all this, the previous government had taken no steps to rectify this ugly situation.

Cows and buffaloes on the road, monkeys in government offices and in residences even in posh colonies and stray dogs at street corners. These are not the hallmarks of a progressive and civilized nation. This menace too has to be tackled forthwith. Animal activists are creating awareness but they must go a step further and take the responsibility to look after them in their own house. You cannot encourage stray dogs and animals on the roadside and in colonies when other residents are unhappy with it. You are free to do what you want but only if you don't transgress on others' rights. Some people in colonies feed strays but will not take them home with the result that other people are very upset and as their children are also scared don't let them play outside. Everyone has equal rights and these rights have to be respected. Feeding of stray animals on the road must be prohibited.

It is not that other countries have become clean without effort. The situation demands not only awareness but also strict rules and penalties against littering and the strictest possible enforcement. I am very happy to note that for the first time an extremely important issue like this has been raised at the level of the Prime Minister of the country. Individual efforts are laudable but they are only like a drop in the ocean but when the will is there at the highest level and the whole program is being turned into a mass movement, this will definitely have fruitful results. Cleanliness is next to godliness and Mr Modi deserves the highest accolades for giving this issue the importance it deserves but which nobody before him deemed fit for attention.

Mr Modi's stress on building toilets also falls into the Swacch Bharat programme. It is high time that open defecation had stopped in India. I have seen even educated men, not very far from public conveniences, just get out of the car and making no attempts to even find a secluded place, relieve themselves on the roadside. This cannot and should not be tolerated any more.

A few more decisions I would place in the same category as the Swacch Bharat campaign. Traffic rules have to be enforced stringently. Compliance does not come without the strictest enforcement. Drivers, driving recklessly, with scant regard for traffic rules, weaving in and out of lanes, flouting speed limits, not only put themselves in danger but create problems for other commuters as well. More traffic jams are created by indiscipline with everyone trying to forge ahead of the other instead of waiting in the queue rather than due to any serious problem. Very often when you finally come out of the traffic jam you wonder why it was there in the first place. There appeared no reason for it. Moreover, shopping areas should be built and no road side shopping on highways should be allowed. These days any thela parks itself just about anywhere on the roadside creating roadblocks.

The government has started talking about cleaning our rivers, the Ganga and the Yamuna. This again is a very laudable step but another area that is in dire need of attention is the cleanliness in and around our temples. One goes to a temple in search of peace, quiet and tranquillity but the experience is the exact opposite. The filth and dirt around, the petty shopkeepers who continuously pester you to buy something or the other for the puja, the beggars who tug at you, the lepers sitting all around, the priests who are no better than beggars themselves and keep exhorting you to give dakshina, the monkeys and cows you have to steer clear of, leave a very bitter taste in the mouth. This is not an experience one looks forward to. Besides this, the milk, the oil, coconuts, the flowers, all combine to create a stench. Anyone starts a temple just about anywhere to collect offerings in cash and kind. It is these practices which don't show Hinduism in a very good light. Our religious leaders must take the lead and bring about reforms which are urgently required. Also we must stop the practice of throwing all kinds of articles in the rivers in the hope that these things carrying all our negative energies will be carried away by the waters. We have reduced our religion to ritualistic practices as against the highest philosophy that is contained in our sacred texts.

The 'Swacch Abhiyan' in my view is a very wide concept. It can cover all aspects of governance. Not only physical but also moral. There is a need for running a Swacch Abhiyan in all fields of administration. Every facet of our life and governance needs to be 'Swacch' or clean and wholesome. Every sector, the electoral, judicial, police, Civil Services, etc, needs a Swacch Abhiyan. First we have to clean up and then only we can build the super structure we all desire. Our minds should also become Swacch and then we can achieve anything. A Swacch Abhiyan will take care of corruption in all spheres. Swacch also means to act sincerely, to maintain principles of justice and fairplay. We must run our Swacch Abhiyan in all sectors.

We should look to the future, cultivate pride in our culture and traditions and become a proud nation holding our own in the world. The country has great hopes from Mr Narendra Modi and he has an extremely difficult job, but as of now he has given Indians the hope that he will deliver on the promises made and much more besides.

Index